HOW TO SURVIVE
A DIVORCE

Allison Jones and Owen Lockwood

ISBN: 1502756269
ISBN 13: 9781502756268
Library of Congress Control Number: 2014918108
CreateSpace Independent Publishing Platform
North Charleston, South Carolina

TABLE OF CONTENTS

DIVORCE IS DIFFICULT

The subject you never thought you would have to think about: divorce. If you have picked up this book it may be time not only to think about it but also to learn as much as you can about the process. It is said that 50 percent of all marriages result in divorce. Although the divorce rate has come down quite a bit in the United States since its all-time high in 1981, it is still alarmingly high. The increase in divorce represents the single most dramatic change in the American family experience during the past fifty years. The large rise in the sheer number of divorces—to over five hundred thousand per year during the 1970s and then to over one million per year during the 1980s—indicates that divorce has now caught up with death as a causal change for marital status in American society. The majority of people who are divorced report that the divorce process was awful. We write this book to try to make this life experience easier. We endeavor to help you make the best of a bad situation. Our hope is that this book will help you survive your legal matters and become a better person through the process. You can go through your divorce or custody case bitter, angry, and resentful, or you can find a way to make the experience one that changes your life for the good. The intent of this book is to help make your experience more positive than negative. No one can eliminate all of the stress and disappointment involved in a divorce or custody dispute, but those experiences can be the catalyst to change your life for the better. It is ultimately your choice.

As you proceed through your legal matter, hopefully it will be increasingly obvious that you can either beat yourself up or choose to see your divorce as a catalyst for building a new life. It is not easy to transform behaviors that no longer serve you, but this is the perfect time to do so. If you don't find and heal the parts of yourself that have kept you from making your marriage work, you will continue to have unhealthy relationships in the future. You may end up divorced a second time or doomed never to love again. If you do not heal the hurt, you are likely to repeat your failures. The center of your focus should be the following: How can I improve myself? What was my contribution to the breakup of my marriage? How can I use this experience to my benefit? How can I use my pain as a motivator to break down the walls that keep old behaviors intact? Don't you want to be a better person, a better parent, and even a better businessperson?

We encourage you to reach out to your attorney, counselor, or parenting class instructor for help with getting started. If you know someone considering a separation, a divorce or facing a custody case, give him or her a copy of this book. It will make the process easier and in some cases maybe even encourage reconciliation. There are great resources and tools in this book to help you put your marriage back together. Even if you cannot save your marriage, you can part as good co-parents or at least not as enemies. If possible, make an exit strategy before you file for divorce. Talk to your attorney, who has helped many people separate in a healthy manner. Make a plan of ways to improve your life and, more importantly, explore ways to finalize your family law matter as quickly as possible. We will discuss all of this later in the book. Our goal is to help you resolve your legal issues as quickly as possible and to save attorney fees along the way. The goal of the legal process is to end the marriage and resolve issues such as:

1.   child custody and support;

2.   visitation;

3.   spousal support, if any;

4.   division of property, assets, and debts; and

5.   payment of legal fees.

A final divorce decree can result from an agreement between the parties or result from trial or arbitration. An agreement is less traumatic for you and your children. Most cases are resolved without a trial. If you reach an agreement you can finalize your divorce on any weekday after the expiration of sixty days from the date your Original Petition for Divorce is filed. If you and your spouse or co-parent cannot reach an agreement, then a Judge will have to make the decision for you. This can take five months or sixteen months—or possibly even longer. We have a divorce in Ft. Bend County, Texas that has been pending for over thirty months, mainly because the prior attorneys and litigants were so acrimonious, and also because the Courts are so crowded.

The manner in which a divorce case is handled as it progresses through the legal system is a major factor in determining how the parties will feel about themselves and each other at the end. The key is figuring out a way to inform your spouse, handle the separation, file the original petition, and get your spouse served without alienating him or her. Separating your emotions from your legal decisions can be very difficult, but you will benefit in the long run. We always recommend that clients find a way to deal with their emotions, whether through counseling, a support group, reading a book or listening to lecture through a webcast or CD.

You should consult a lawyer if your marriage seems to be ending. Even if you are unsure about divorcing and you want your marriage to work, you should still see an attorney. The ultimate outcome of the divorce process can be significantly affected by how the process is initiated, and there are a lot of things you can do before you actually file for divorce that can make the process go more smoothly. An attorney can give you information about the divorce process and advise you about your rights to custody, property and support. Your lawyer can also prepare a separation agreement if you are not ready to file for divorce. You need assurance that timely steps are being taken to obtain a divorce, and you need someone to advise you when unexpected problems arise. Your lawyer can also seek protection if your spouse threatens to assault or harass you or take your children in violation of a custody agreement. While Texas does not have legal separation, we can prepare a separation agreement so both parties can agree to abide by certain rules while they are deciding how to proceed. See chapter 40 on alternatives to divorce.

This book is set out in chapters. If you just want to read about a specific subject, you can turn directly to the chapter on that topic. For example, arbitration is covered in chapter 10. When we refer to your attorney, we will say *he or she*. This is in the interest of having a text that is gender neutral. We believe there are more female family law lawyers than male, but we will use *he, she* or *your attorney* when we refer to an attorney.

The information regarding Texas law provided in this book is current as of the date that this book is was published in 2015. The laws in Texas are regularly updated and changed. You should consult an attorney to advise you on the current status of Texas law when proceeding through the process of a divorce. You may also look at the website for this book for updates. Our website is: howtosurviveadivorce.net

Chapter 1

HIRING A LAW FIRM

When hiring your divorce attorney, please interview at least two attorneys to make sure you have the confidence and the trust in them that is necessary to get through this process. Within the first thirty minutes, you can easily tell if you click with the attorney. If you have reservations, discuss your concerns with the potential attorney or interview another attorney. Make sure the caseload of the attorney you hire is at least 50 percent family law. In smaller counties this may not be possible, but make sure that the attorney is one who practices family law on a regular basis and, if possible, one who is board certified in family law. If you need a referral to an attorney in Texas who has a holistic approach to resolving family matters, please e-mail us at info@familylawoffices.com with the county, court number, and opposing counsel (if any), and we will be happy to send you referrals.

When selecting an attorney, make sure that attorney's values are aligned with yours. Do you want to go through a healing process or a battle? Some people want a battle, while others want to avoid conflict at all costs and want to finalize as soon as possible. You need to discuss this with your attorney at the first interview. The emotional toll of going through a divorce can affect people in serious and sometimes unexpected ways. We have seen many extreme examples of how the stress and emotions involved in going through a divorce can impact people and cause them to behave in unexpected ways. This is why selecting the right attorney to help you through the process can make a huge difference in how the process affects you in the long run.

If you offer as much compassion as possible for all parties involved, especially for your soon-to-be-ex-spouse or parent of your children, the legal process will be less expensive, proceed more quickly, and you will be able to begin the healing process much sooner. This may not seem obtainable at the outset. But if you make it your main focus and discuss it with your attorney, you will be surprised at how quickly you can recover. Make sure your attorney is on board with your intentions. We realize revenge can be sweet, but often it backfires and sets you back to square one—or an even a worse position.

The following are examples of situations we counsel our clients against indulging in:

A wife going through a nasty separation took a seam ripper to her husband's business suits to take out the seam in the rear end of six pairs of his pants. At four different high-level oil company meetings, his pants split when he bent down or reached up, exposing his rear end. We often wonder why the husband did not realize the prank after his pants ripped the second time. The wife was later reprimanded by the court and had to replace all six of his business suits. If you do not deal with your anger or disappointment, it will destroy you. The next case is in the crossover group between mean and sad. The husband, whose wife had had a double mastectomy, was a doctor. His wife had put him through medical school, after which he left her and married his nurse. In response to her need for reconstructive surgery, he said, "I'm not paying for her boob job." The court ordered him to pay the bills for the reconstructive surgery and gave the wife 58 percent of the marital estate.

Besides the embarrassment and shame the good doctor endured in going to trial, he ended up paying her an additional $230,000.

Even when you know that getting a divorce is the right thing to do, you will almost certainly experience a wide range of emotions as you go through the process. We try to help our clients legally, emotionally, and mentally by giving them the right tools and resources to help them become better people. Getting stuck or struggling with anger or guilt will eat you up alive. No attorney has all the solutions on for emotional issues, but your attorney can help you set up a plan and refer you to the right people.

The Kübler-Ross Model, or the five stages of grief, is a series of emotional stages we experience when faced with impending death or a life-altering event. This model was first introduced by Swiss American psychiatrist Elizabeth Kübler-Ross in her 1965 book, *Death and Dying*, which is based on her experience working with terminally ill patients. The stages are denial, anger, bargaining, depression, and acceptance. Kübler-Ross noted that these stages are not meant to be a complete list of all possible emotions that could be felt, and they can occur in any order. Her model can equally apply to separation and divorce. In divorce it is normal to go through denial, anger, bargaining, guilt, and depression. So, if you are angry or depressed, you can take some comfort in knowing that you'll probably feel differently in a few weeks. Divorce is stressful, but it is not the end of the world. You get to decide how long you will stay in the anger, denial, or guilt stage. Holding anger for your spouse or the parent of your children is like taking poison yourself and hoping the other person will die. It makes no sense. Hopefully you will achieve the final freedom that comes from forgiveness. The antidote for anger is forgiveness.

Everyone goes through this at a different pace, and some people cope better with stress than others. Talking with a counselor about how to deal with stress is often helpful. Counseling can help you see emotional issues for what they are so that you can make better judgments as to legal and financial matters. Lawyers are not trained to do counseling, so seeing a therapist would be helpful. Counseling can help you and your spouse understand the reasons and causes of the marital breakup. You need to understand what went wrong with this marriage to help you to have better relationships in the future. You should also consider counseling or support classes for your children. Many children have trouble dealing with divorce. They are frightened and feel responsible. The Escape Family Resource Center (713-942-9500) and the Deplechin Children's Center (281-730-2335) offer classes for children that often take place at the same time adults take their mandatory four-hour parenting class.

At our law firm, our values are the rules by which we operate: be fair, be honest, be a good listener, respect the individual, encourage intellectual curiosity, and contribute to the community. We vow to approach all family law matters in a holistic manner so that our clients experience the least amount of collateral damage.

If you have hired or plan to hire our firm, thank you. We handle most matters in the family law area: child custody, adoptions, divorce, litigation, modifications and enforcement of orders, postnuptial agreements, and prenuptial contracts. For some of the most specialized areas, such as artificial reproduction, gestation agreements and enforcements, we will be happy to give you a referral. Our firm handles approximately 95 percent family matters; the remaining 5 percent consists of civil and corporate clients. The majority of our clients have been fathers fighting for custody, but our firm represents husbands, wives, mothers, fathers, and grandparents. We do not specialize with a particular gender. It has just worked out that the majority of our trials have involved fathers fighting for custody. We also handle a lot of property trials. To get to know our firm, please review our resumes on our website at www.familylawoffices.com.

Once you have hired your attorney, it is inevitable that you will develop an extremely close relationship with him or her. You will need to tell us everything. You may tell us more intimate details than you have shared with your best friend or your counselor. You must have trust in the lawyer you hire or the process will be much harder and more expensive.

The most common reason for litigation in the family law area is lack of communication between the parties. This holds true in any professional relationship as well, which includes your relationship with your attorney. Therefore, please make every effort to keep the lines of communication open if you have any concerns about the legal process. In order to ensure a productive working relationship, please bring your concerns to your attorney's attention immediately. It isn't possible to fix a problem that isn't brought to light. We believe it is your lawyer's job to eliminate stress from your life, not to add to it. If you are having a hard time getting in touch with your attorney, try to make an appointment with his or her legal assistant. If that does not help or answer your questions, ask to set up a twenty-minute telephone conference with the attorney. Write your questions down before placing the call. Have your documents in front of you during the call and make notes. Try to make a to-do list every time you talk to your attorney's office. Repeat it back to your attorney at the end of the call or appointment. The two most important documents in a divorce are your proposed property division and the proposed parenting plan. If you take notes on the proposed property division or proposed parenting plan during the call or meeting with your attorney or legal assistant, you will understand the process better.

Lawyers work on many cases at a time, and the practice of family law requires lawyers to spend time in court, at depositions, in conferences, and on the telephone. So you should not expect your lawyer to always be available when you call. You should, however, expect that either your lawyer or a staff member will respond to your messages promptly. If an emergency arises, tell the person who answers the telephone that it is an emergency and explain the situation. Likewise, if your attorney calls and leaves a message for you to call back, you should do so as soon as possible. Your lawyer will appreciate your calling during regular business hours, unless it is a real emergency.

We discuss the quickest and least expensive way to get client questions answered in our office, and we hope your attorney's office is similar. If you e-mail your questions, we try to answer all e-mails within twenty-four hours—usually the same day. The attorneys in our office are often in mediation or court, so you *must* send a copy of your message to the legal assistant assigned to your case. If your attorney's office does not follow this procedure, please ask the legal assistant for the best way to get your questions answered.

If you are concerned that nothing is happening in your case, talk to the attorney, the legal assistant, or the office manager. At our office, all concerns should be directed to our office manager, who can resolve most problems that arise. You are entitled to know the status of your case. There may be a good reason for a delay. But you need to know the reason and what the next step is. If you cannot get answers from the legal assistant, ask the office manager. If that does not work, make an appointment with the attorney. If you cannot get an answer, write a letter; if that doesn't work, you may need to switch attorneys. Feel free to call the office any time you have questions or concerns about your case. In order to keep your fees to a minimum, please speak with the legal assistant assigned to your case, but remember you can speak to or meet with an attorney at any time; all you have to do is ask. Your message should quickly be relayed to one of the attorneys. Feel comfortable in communicating with the legal assistant, as they have the same responsibility regarding confidentiality as the attorneys do. One of an attorney's most fundamental ethical obligations is to maintain the confidentiality of client communication. Your attorney is prohibited from revealing anything learned while representing you. These rules exist so you can tell your attorney the truth without fear that it will be used against you. There are two exceptions to the attorney-client privilege: child abuse and a client's intention to commit a crime. Every law office member must report all child abuse to law enforcement officials. In our office, we return all calls within twenty-four hours, usually within the same day unless it is a weekend and nonemergency. If the attorneys are in court, depositions, or an appointment, please leave a phone number and the best time to return your call. The legal assistant may be able to answer your question if an attorney is not available. You may also fax or e-mail your questions or concerns, and we will respond within twenty-four hours. Our office manager will gladly schedule a specific time for you to speak with one of the attorneys in person or by telephone conference within forty-eight hours.

People can represent themselves in a divorce case. A person who represents himself or herself is called a *pro se litigant*. A *pro se litigant* must follow the same rules as an attorney, including the rules of procedure, evidence, and the local rules. The rules that apply in a family law case can be complicated and confusing. We recommend consulting legal aid services available in your community and, if you have the means to do so, hiring an attorney to assist you. In Harris County, the phone number for Lone Star Legal Aid is 713-652-0077 or 800-733-8394.

Chapter 2

ATTORNEY'S FEES

Divorce makes everybody poorer—at least initially. When the same income that was supporting one household is now responsible for maintaining two households, plus attorney's fees for two different attorneys, there is rarely enough income to cover the additional expense. A recent study found that three-fifths of men and three-quarters of women underwent significant declines in their standard of living commencing abruptly after separation. Men usually rebound faster. The adverse long-term economic ramifications of divorce are much worse for women. Only about 15 percent of divorced women nationwide are awarded alimony. In Texas, it is much less. Those women who are entitled to receive money following their divorce have a hard time collecting it. Of those women who get divorced and are entitled to child support payments, only about three-fourths actually receive them, and only half receive full payment. Most women in Texas cannot expect spousal support to save the day. Please read Chapter 28 for more on spousal support.

There are two dramatically different types of divorce cases that can be processed through the family courts. Your divorce can be either contested or uncontested. If you are able to achieve an uncontested divorce, you reap the many benefits: (1) you save a lot of money; (2) you avoid a lot of stress;

(3) you get your divorce completed within two to three months; and (4) you salvage some sort of decent relationship with your former spouse. This issue is especially important when you have children.

Let's start with the scary issues: getting sued, getting divorced, or getting arrested. These are likely foreign processes to you, so the legal system may be somewhat intimidating. That is normal. Most people only go to court once or twice in their entire lives, and entering the process can be overwhelming. The way to alleviate this is to learn as much as possible about the process. This book will assist you. How do you get the help you need without paying more than you should? It is impossible to predict how much your divorce will cost, although your lawyer may be able to give you a range. The cost of the case depends on many factors, some of which are beyond your lawyer's control. These factors include the kind of lawyer your spouse hires, how you and your spouse behave in the litigation and the court to which your case is assigned. Generally, the more things you and your spouse can agree on, the lower your fees will be. There is a lot you can do to help keep the fees down. Be actively involved in your case. Take the time to learn what's going on. Follow your lawyer's instructions. Volunteer to help with the work whenever possible. Have reasonable expectations of your lawyer. Watch for ways to settle issues. Don't insist on fighting to the last drop of blood over small issues or for a supposed principle. When talking to your lawyer, avoid long, detailed stories unless your lawyer assures you it's necessary information. It is often much more efficient to write a history for your attorney. Make sure you pick your battles, and only fight if you have tried all other options offered by your attorney. It is important to get the attorneys out of the parties' lives to stop the accumulation of attorney's fees as soon as possible and get back to the "new norm."

The biggest factor in keeping your costs down is you. You must understand that it is usually smarter and less expensive to settle litigation out of court. There are exceptions. But they are called exceptions for a reason; they are rare. When you feel victimized by your spouse, you may want to go to battle. You may want your spouse to pay for what he or she has done. We hear complaints like these very often: she cheated on me; I don't want the divorce; now I am being kicked out of my house; I have to pay $1,710 in child support every month and give him half of my retirement; how can that be fair? These feelings are normal, and you need to work through them without obsessing over them. Thinking deeply about a problem is good, but when you keep thinking about it over and over, that is rumination. Another definition of ruminate is "when an animal chews his cud over and over then swallows it, digests it, and then throws it all up and starts the process all over again." When you overthink a problem, it keeps looping repeatedly through your mind. This is quite common in divorce. Some normal concerns one could feel overly worried about are these: (1) Will I have to move, or lose my house or my car? (2) Will I have enough money to support myself and the kids? (3) How will the kids adjust from spending thirty days with their father?

So how do you find the right balance between properly processing all the changes and constantly thinking about them? Hopefully your parents, counselor, pastor, best friend, or parenting coordinator can help you through the process. Don't hesitate to ask for help or direction. The biggest mistake people make in going through a divorce or a custody battle is not going to counseling because they think it will make them look bad in court. They believe if they go to a counselor it will hurt their chances of getting custody or that it will make them appear weak. This is untrue.

It is impossible to predict with certainty how long out-of-court disputes will take to resolve. But an experienced lawyer should have a good idea. Most cases in our office are resolved within three to six months. Don't be afraid to speak frankly to your attorney about your desire to keep his or her fees to a minimum. Your attorney should be on your side. Several divorces that we have recently taken over have been pending for two years because the parties want to fight and do not want to let go. So how long your divorce takes to finalize depends a lot on how you and your spouse behave.

In most cases, each party in a divorce pays his or her own legal fees. In some cases, however, one spouse may be ordered to reimburse the other for legal fees or a portion of the fees. You should discuss this with your attorney at the beginning of your case.

Procedures and Billing for the Law Office

Knowing how an attorney bills will help you prevent spending unnecessary money and give you some peace of mind. Lawyers (like brokers, bankers, and insurance agents) are service providers. You hire them to solve problems and achieve goals. If a lawyer does good work, he or she helps the client accumulate and protect wealth. An attorney who does shoddy work can put the client in financial danger. When the attorney charges more than is appropriate, the situation worsens. That is why it is so important to select your attorney carefully.

A good lawyer will let you know in advance that fighting is costly. Your attorney should encourage you to be realistic about your divorce. If you've found a good lawyer, he or she will manage your expectations. Many clients ask if we can make their spouse pay for their fees. As stated above, a court may order a spouse to contribute to the fees of the other spouse. If you get such an order, your lawyer will credit what is actually paid to your account. But seeking such an order does not change your obligation to pay the balance that you owe to your own lawyer. Also, many lawyers do not accept cases on the possibility that the other spouse will be required to pay the fee after mediation or trial. Remember that you would have to go to trial in order for the court to award fees.

If you give the legal assistant information, please do not call back and tell the attorney the same details. When you send duplicate information or e-mails, it will increase the attorney's fees. We have to open the new e-mail and compare it to e-mail you sent a few days ago so we don't miss anything. This is time-consuming. If you are confused or unsure about what your attorney has received, make an appointment with the legal assistant assigned to your case and go over the status. You are welcome to meet with the attorney any time, but you can reduce attorney fees by meeting with the legal assistant for an hour and the attorney for the last fifteen minutes of the appointment. When you are compiling your documents to respond to discovery (discussed in more detail in chapter 12), you should definitely meet with the legal assistant to keep your attorney fees to a minimum.

To view an example of a contract, the contract for our office is on our website. It's a fairly standard contract for attorney fees. A law office charges hourly for the time spent on your case, whether it is a telephone call, meetings, travel, drafting, correspondence, or court appearances. Before work can begin on your case, you must return the signed contact and pay the initial retainer.

You can help your attorney's office keep fees to a minimum by paying your bill in a timely manner. You will generally receive an invoice on the first day of each month or early in each month. (See Exhibit 4 for an example of an invoice). Please review the statement carefully. If you have questions regarding the charges, please call the financial manager or accounting office within fifteen days of receipt of the invoice. Payment in full is expected at the time the invoice is received. When you pay your initial retainer, we place the funds in a trust account and use those funds for payment of the fees you incur. You will be responsible for replenishing your account and maintaining the minimum balance agreed upon in the contract. Additional funds will be required for mediation, deposition, hearings, and trial.

In an effort to keep attorney's fees down, we encourage you to use some or all of the following suggestions:

1. Save all questions for one call whenever possible; keep a list of your questions and have them with you when you contact your attorney.

2. Ask to speak to a legal assistant first. Most of the time, the legal assistant can help you with questions and problems, which in turn can cut your legal fees in half. Bear in mind, however, that legal assistants cannot give legal advice. If the legal assistant cannot answer a question, he or she will have the attorney call or e-mail you with the answer.

3. Use e-mail for as many of your questions as possible. Attorneys, legal assistants, and other staff members typically check messages throughout the day.

4. You may also communicate via facsimile with some firms. This can be an additional way to communicate new developments in your case.

5. In custody disputes, keep a diary called *attorney-client updates*. Do not share this with anyone but your counselor or your attorney. E-mail or fax this update weekly if possible.

6. Do not throw away any financial records or other potential exhibits. Do not destroy e-mails or erase your text messages during the pendency of the divorce.

7. Create a timeline. It will help the attorney and legal assistant organize your case. It will also help keep everyone focused on the right issues and help keep fees down while preparing for trial. In a custody case, you can give your

timeline to the amicus attorney for the child, the mental health evaluator, or the social worker.

You have hired an attorney to act as your representative. At our firm, we promise to go above and beyond the call of duty to resolve your family law matter, incurring the least amount of attorney fees. We will always keep the best interest of the children foremost. We will strive to obtain the best property division for you in the quickest amount of time possible without compromising quality. On a recent case handled by our firm, the mother of two girls, ages twelve and sixteen, wanted to divorce quickly and "keep the attorney fees to a minimum." She hired us at the end of the Summer and wanted her divorce finalized before Christmas. She called to ask why the divorce was not finalized and why we had billed her $7,800 for the discovery process. We were able to uncover an $80,000 bonus and stock options worth over $100,000, of which she received half. The divorce was finalized in the Spring, two months after she wanted, but she received an extra $90,000. The husband in that case has referred his friends to our firm—not the attorney that represented him, but his wife's attorney. We don't know if the husband failed to disclose the assets innocently or if he was trying to cheat his wife out of her half of the $180,000. We will never know. In some cases it will be necessary to hire a certified forensic accountant to examine the financial records and to see if there is any missing or hidden money. It would be this accountant's job to reconstruct the parties' finances and find any hidden assets.

A good firm will make no representations, promises, or guarantees as to the outcome of your case. You must agree to pay for legal services based upon the time expended by the attorney or staff members. This may include, but is not limited to: conferences, court appearances, mediation, settlement conferences, negotiations, preparation of documents, and travel. You will be asked to pay an additional trial retainer if your case does not settle. Since you are buying the attorney's time, which includes his or her experience and perseverance, it isn't possible to know how much time you will need to purchase in order to finish your case. Most uncontested divorces take between five to ten hours of an attorney's time and ten to fifteen hours of a legal assistant's time. Our office has completed some uncontested divorces for as little as $1,500 (not including filing fees)—but not many. Most uncontested divorces, excluding court fees, cost between $2,500 and $10,000.

People will fight over the silliest things. In a recent divorce case, a couple fought over a breast pump and a crib. We often wonder what the husband wanted with the breast pump. In another case, the couple spent thousands of dollars fighting over a fondue set. Again, it would have been a lot cheaper to have purchased a new one. The winner of the most trivial property dispute is the husband who filed a postdivorce suit to divide an undivided asset, his former wife's shoes. We have had trials over custody of a pet and a horse, as well as visitation rights for the family dog, but usually it is best to avoid trial for these disputes.

After signing the contract and paying the retainer fee, your original petition for Divorce should be filed within two days unless you specify otherwise, depending on your exit strategy and when you want to serve your spouse. If you do not receive a copy of the contract and the original petition for divorce within five days, please notify your attorney's office. Your spouse or the opposing party will then be notified that the divorce has been filed. In Harris County, Texas, this takes approximately ten days, depending on the district clerk's workload.

Chapter 3

SEPARATION AND FILING FOR DIVORCE

The first step in the divorce process is separation. In this part of the process, you will need to decide how to tell your spouse you are moving forward with the divorce or deal with the fact that you have just received this news from your spouse. This is a big step, and how it is handled can have a huge impact on how your case proceeds. Whenever possible, we encourage people to tell their spouse through a handwritten letter or, if appropriate, a conversation in person. Many times, giving your spouse a letter that describes your decisions and gives them a chance to have a weekend to themselves to process the information helps get the situation moving in a way that prevents unnecessary hostility. Sometimes this is not possible because of a history of violence in the relationship. In those cases, we focus on the safety of our client and the children, if any, and we will find a separation strategy to ensure the safety of everyone involved. All married couples go through this process in different ways. Some separations are amicable and the parties are able to communicate well. This makes the divorce process easier on everyone and saves a lot of money in the form of attorney's fees. If you have an attorney at this stage of the process, we recommend talking to him or her about the process of separation to develop a healthy exit plan.

When you are considering divorce, you need to make sure that you have access to all of your important information that you will need during the divorce process. You should make copies of the following documents and keep them in a safe place:

1. Income tax returns with all W-2s, 1099s, and all other reported income for the past three years

2. Your spouse's most recent pay stub, as well as the name, address, and phone number of the employer

3. Your spouse's driver's license and social security number

4. Titles, registration, and loan documents for all vehicles

5. Deeds and loan documents for all properties

6. Wills, life insurance policies, pensions, and retirement account statements

7. Health and dental insurance policies and cards

8. Bank and credit card statements for all accounts

9. Statements for all brokerage accounts, retirement accounts and other investment accounts.

You should start gathering information as early as possible. If there is a sudden separation, you may find yourself in a position where you cannot obtain this information at a later date. You will also need to have this information available for your attorney when you meet with him or her. You may also want to gather sentimental items such as the children's baby books, your family's jewelry, or your diary to prevent your spouse holding these items hostage.

When children are involved, one of the most important considerations is how to tell them about the divorce. How you and your future ex-spouse go about telling your children should depend on their age and maturity. Telling your children as a couple can have a lot of benefits. It conveys an idea that this is a mutual decision and that they will still have two parents. It is nearly impossible to predict how children will react to this news, so be prepared to handle a range of reactions. Reading a book with your children, or giving them one to read, may help the process. Some books that are available are the following:

> *The Divorced Helpbook for Teens*,
> by Cynthia MacGregor

> *How It Feels When Parents Divorce*,
> by Jill Krementz.

> *My Parents Are Divorced Too: A Book for Kids by Kids*,
> by Melanie Ford.

Before you file for a divorce in Texas, you must meet the residency requirement, which is six months as of the date this book was written. You must have resided in Texas for the preceding six months and in the County where you are filing for divorce for the preceding ninety days. The following information and instructions apply generally to all divorce cases in Texas, although they will differ slightly from county to county. Your attorney will inform you whenever it is necessary for you to be in the office, to sign legal documents, to attend conferences, or to appear in court. Please understand that if at any time you find it necessary to discuss this case with an attorney or legal assistant, you should make an appointment as soon as possible.

Here, we will explain the commencement of a divorce and temporary relief prior to an agreement or trial. The divorce usually begins with the service of the following legal documents:

1. The petition for divorce (referred to as Original Petition or OP). This basically sets forth the names of the parties, children, date of marriage, date of separation, and a request for the court to grant the divorce. The first person to file is called the petitioner. We are often asked, "Should I be the first to file?" Generally it does not matter. It can matter if child custody is at issue and in a few other situations but most of the time, it does not matter who files first. In most cases, your attorney will file a counterpetition to request certain relief so that you will, in essence, have the same rights as the petitioner. In this situation you will be called a counter-petitioner.

    "Why did my spouse ask for so much in the petition? I thought we agreed on some of those things." Before knowing what the issues will be and what might happen under the law and the facts of the case, no one wants to take the chance of asking for too little. For this reason, many attorneys tend to ask for more than the client really expects. Newspapers may report that someone has filed a $10 million divorce suit, but what is demanded in the petition usually has little meaning in the end. Do not get upset if you get served with an original petition requesting that you have limited visitation and that you pay 100 percent of the legal fees.

2. Request for Temporary Orders. Often an original petition is accompanied with a request for Temporary Relief. This is basically a request to the court that some temporary rules be established to govern issues with your children and the use of money and property while the divorce is pending. This usually includes an affidavit supporting the request for temporary relief, which is the basis for obtaining a court

setting, and which must be specific in laying out the details of your circumstances and what you are requesting the court to do. The order requested may include temporary provisions for the following relief: support payments for either party, support for the minor children, removal of a spouse from the home, determination of who shall have temporary custody of the minor children, and a determination of who shall make mortgage payments and meet other obligations while the action is pending. The order to show cause (appear and present evidence relevant to temporary orders) contains the date of the hearing before a family court judge and the request for temporary relief. Many cases do not need a temporary order hearing. This hearing is usually held within three to five weeks after the OP is filed.

3.   Citation and notice of the hearing.You must notify the other party that a suit for divorce has been filed. You may do this by having a process server serve the opposing party with a citation, which is a document prepared by the District Clerk's Office, with the original petition for divorce attached, and the notice of the hearing if you have requested temporary orders. As an alternative, you may have the opposing party sign a waiver of citation if he or she will agree to accept the documents informally and does not want a process server to serve them.

If you have been served with a petition for divorce, you need to seek advice from an attorney immediately. If you don't respond to the petition within a specified time frame, you risk losing your ability to present your side of the case or the ability to contest any of the issues in the divorce. Consulting with an attorney as soon as possible will help you to preserve your rights. In

Texas you have until the Monday after the expiration of twenty days from the date you are served to file an answer.

Temporary Restraining Order

Filing for a temporary restraining order (TRO) when it is not necessary may cause the early stages of the divorce to be much more contentious than they should be. If you need to file a temporary restraining order, temporary mutual injunctions, and permanent injunctions, talk to your attorney. Injunctions are used to restrain inappropriate behavior. The following is an example of the types of behaviors that parties may be prohibited from in a temporary restraining order:

1. Disturbing the peace of the children or of another party

2. Withdrawing the children from enrollment in the school or day-care facility where the children are presently enrolled

3. Hiding or secreting the children from the other party

4. Making disparaging remarks regarding the other party or the other party's family in the presence or within the hearing of the children

5. Discussing any aspects of the divorce with the children

If the conflict between you and your spouse becomes so intense that you cannot resolve it on your own, then request that the court grant a temporary restraining order good for approximately fourteen to twenty-eight days. The TRO can then be converted into a temporary or permanent mutual injunction. The court usually requires that the majority of the injunctions be mutual to both parties.

The specifics of how your case will play out are difficult to determine in advance. Every case is different, and a lot depends on how the opposing party responds. This is a basic outline of how a divorce or custody case generally proceeds.

Divorce Process Flow Chart

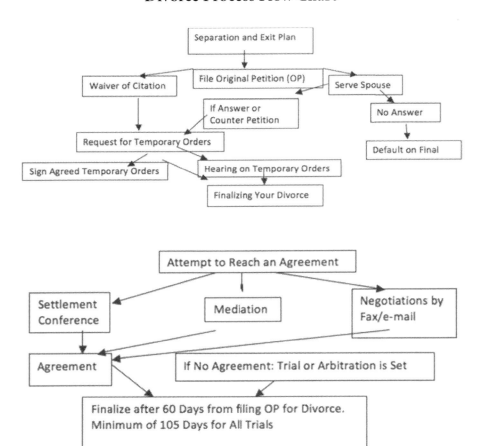

Chapter 4

TEMPORARY ORDERS HEARING

Temporary orders set the rules while the case is pending. Either party can ask the court to set a temporary hearing. If your case needs temporary orders in place, these orders can be established through a number of ways. In many cases, temporary orders are established by agreement of the parties and then prepared in a written order that the judge will sign. Sometimes, parties will attend mediation to resolve any disputes on temporary orders. In some cases, establishing temporary orders requires a hearing in court so that the judge can issue a set of orders when the parties cannot reach an agreement.

It is best for both parties to agree upon reasonable arrangements while the case is pending rather than incur additional attorney's legal fees and increase the level of animosity. If you and your spouse (or parent of your child) cannot reach an agreement on temporary orders, such as who will live in the house, who will have custody, who will pay child support or visitation, then the court will decide.

A temporary orders hearing is the opportunity for the parties to present evidence to the court so that the temporary rules that will be in place can be decided if there is no agreement. Temporary orders typically address issues such as temporary custody of the children, terms for visitation with the children, temporary child support, temporary spousal support, and who has the right to the use of certain marital property while the case is pending. In addition, the court may order a set of injunctions that the parties must abide by during the divorce process. Temporary injunctions are basically a list of behavior that the parties are ordered not to engage in while the case is pending. These typically include orders relating to the handling of property and how the parties are supposed to act toward each other while the case is pending. Well in advance of any hearings or trial, you will meet with the legal assistant or attorney to prepare for your court hearing. Consider bringing a video recorder to record yourself while testifying in any rehearsal or practice session.

If your case requires a temporary orders hearing, you need to take this hearing very seriously. This is when you present your case to the court regarding what you want to happen while your case is pending. You need to be as prepared as possible. You also need to bring as much evidence as possible to the temporary orders hearing because important issues in the case, like custody and use of marital residence, will be determined at this hearing and may have a bearing on the final outcome.

Chapter 5

CONFLICT AND COOPERATION

Conflict between spouses who are divorcing is inevitable. The conflict may be a carryover from the marriage, a long time dysfunctional pattern, or a result from one spouse's anger toward the other for leaving. Conflict between the parties is not necessary. Attorneys do their best to advise clients in how to prevent conflicts. There's an old saying among attorneys, "Criminal lawyers represent some truly horrible people who, when in court, are on their very best behavior. Divorce lawyers represent ordinarily very nice people who happen to be acting their absolute worst during the divorce." Frankly, frayed nerves are so common among dissolving couples that virtually every horrible behavior imaginable can, and does, occur during their divorce. This behavior often stems from a sense of hurt, shame, or helplessness.

You Benefit from Cooperation between the Lawyers

Agreements called stipulations can be reached that simplify the case, move it toward settlement, and save you money. Lawyers often meet without their clients to try to isolate areas of agreement and at the same time will still vigorously represent you in court. Additionally, the time spent exchanging information and negotiating will make you and your lawyer better prepared for a settlement conference, mediation, or trial.

Lawyers routinely extend simple courtesies to each other, such as agreeing to extend deadlines and postpone hearings. You may feel like every advantage should be pressed in your favor, and that if the other side is under time pressure, your lawyer should take advantage of it. But in the long run, it doesn't help you if your lawyer is uncooperative. In most cases, an extension is available by court order anyway. Refusing to agree just costs you and your spouse more legal fees, and don't forget that the shoe will be on the other foot someday. When you need more time, you don't want the other side to be inspired by a past discourtesy and refuse. Then you will have to go to court for relief and your legal fees will again increase. Still, you are not powerless in these matters. If you truly believe that a delay will work to your detriment, tell your lawyer so that you can discuss what to do. Finally, it is important for lawyers to treat each other in a way that makes it possible to work together in all cases. The good reputation your lawyer has developed for cooperation and reasonableness in previous cases will benefit you in your case.

Cooperation between Parents

Many parents can minimize the conflict or at least keep it away from the children. Your number one goal should be to become good co-parents. It may seem difficult at this stage, but it is well worth it. Your children will benefit. Many times the high level of conflict will reduce substantially once the parents start living apart, and it will reduce again once the divorce is granted. Even nonverbal children can sense the negative energy between their parents and be affected by it.

"Parental conflict predicts less father involvement, ultimately affecting young children's early socialization and acquisition of necessary life skills." Pruett et al., "Family and Legal Indicators of Child

Adjustment to Divorce Among Families with Young Children," *J. Fam. Psychol.* 17 (2003): 169, 176.

If you use language of anger, you will continue to hold anger. This hurts you the most! Do not refer to your ex-husband as "the ex" or similar name, because it shows the children your lack of respect for their father. Call him what he is, if talking to the kids—"your father," or use "the father of my children," if talking with other adults. Be sensitive to the language and words you use with the children. As an example, if you say, "Let's get ready; you *have* to go to your father's," depending on how you emphasize the words "you have," you could be putting a negative thought in their minds. We are not suggesting you say, "Yippee, you get to go to your father's," but there are many ways to turn the statement into a positive. Anger, if not used to motivate constructive behavior, only saps your energy and causes disease. How you act and what you say during the divorce affects your children. Your conduct makes a big difference in how your children feel and how they relate to their other parent.

Cooperating during the divorce can set the tone for how you and the other parent will work together in the future for your children's welfare. Even after you are divorced, you are still the parents of your children. Their best interests are served if each of you is courteous to the other and maintains an active role in the lives of the children. If you and your spouse are not able to put aside your differences and put the children first, the children will suffer. You can decide not to be bitter, even if your spouse left you for a younger woman or a wealthier man, there is no benefit to remaining bitter.

Many clients ask, "May I date?" In some courts, your private life is not a concern. In others, a relationship with someone other than your spouse before you are divorced may hurt your case. Dating someone else may anger your spouse and impede settlement. It is hard to get cooperation from your spouse when you have already moved on and the divorce is not even finalized. If you have children, you should get some professional advice about how much your children should know about your love life. Do not introduce your children to your new boyfriend or girlfriend before your divorce is finalized under any circumstances. Please tell your attorney if you have had an affair early on. For your own sake, discuss the situation with your attorney or legal assistant before you start dating.

Co-Parenting Tools

Our Family Wizard and Custody Junction Co-parenting website are great programs that can eliminate stress and miscommunication. These programs generally cost between forty-five and one hundred dollars per parent, based on 2014 pricing plans. The Family Wizard has an "attitude check," much like spell check. It will suggest other ways to word something if it detects sarcasm or rudeness.

One of our client's passwords at the bank was "I hate John." While we laughed when she told us, it was really sad. Although her child was only eighteen months old, and wouldn't understand even if she heard the password, it would still affect her. Again, if you use language of anger you will continue to hold anger. Children can sense your mood before you even realize it. Have you ever had your child ask what is wrong? Even though you may have replied that nothing was wrong, you may have been shocked at how perceptive they were. You had not realized you were upset or agitated until your child brought it to your attention.

Chapter 6

AFTER TEMPORARY ORDERS

After any necessary temporary orders have been resolved, your case will start moving through the finalization process. This part of the process can last for only a couple of months or for a couple of years or more. The amount of time your case takes to finalize depends on a lot of factors, but the most important is the behavior of the parties.

General Instructions

1. Follow all court orders explicitly. If you have questions, call the legal assistant assigned to your case to make sure you understand your rights and responsibilities.

2. If you have custody of your children, have them appropriately dressed and ready for visitation at the arranged times. Do not present obstacles to visitation if your spouse is not cooperative about making Court Ordered payments. You cannot deny the other parent visitation simply because they are behind in their child support.

3.   If you have visitation rights, be there to pick up your children and return them on time.

4.   Do not alienate the children from your spouse. This is a most trying time for the children. Do not discuss your marital problems with them. They should not feel a necessity to side with either parent. Children should love both parents. Anything that you can do to make visitation more pleasant will benefit them.

5.   If you are making payments, pay promptly and as ordered. If it is impossible for you to do so, notify your attorney immediately. If you are required to make payments through the State Disbursement Unit, *do not* make payments directly to your spouse.

6.   If a change in circumstances occurs, such as a layoff, a substantial reduction in pay, an accident, an emergency, unexpected medical or dental problems, please contact your attorney immediately, as he or she must be aware of these things to serve you best.

7.   Do not argue with your spouse. Any important problems should be brought to the attorney.

8.   Discuss your divorce with your attorney, not with others, even though they may inquire. Their advice is not grounded in proper training and consequently is likely to be inaccurate, even when based upon their personal experiences. Their circumstances may be far different from yours or the laws may have changed. It is like using another's eyeglasses: they rarely fit properly. When a friend or family member wants to tell you about the other parent,

shut them off immediately. You can say, "I want to get through this divorce in a healthy manner, wallowing in that gossip will not help. If you think it is important to my case, please call my attorney. But as much as I want to hear it, I must insist you stop, and do not share with me anything about my ex-spouse."

9. Inform your attorney promptly of changes in phone numbers, addresses, or employment status.

10. If you believe that there is a chance for reconciliation, contact your attorney immediately. He or she can have the court suspend the action, which can be done for ninety days or more, depending on the court to which you are assigned.

We understand that this is a most difficult time for you. Each case is different as is each human being. Attorneys cannot predict what you need to get through this process. Make sure you tell your attorney if you need to meet with him. Do not wait for the law office to call you to set up an appointment. If you have a question or are concerned, please e-mail your attorney's office about your concerns or questions. This should help to clear your concerns. If it doesn't, call the office to set up an appointment. Attorneys expect you to keep them informed of important matters, and they likewise will keep you informed of important developments affecting your case.

Scheduling Order

The Harris County Courts have adopted a system to prevent cases from becoming "stale" in the system. After a case has been pending for approximately six to nine months, the court issues a scheduling order that assigns a trial date and dates for compliance with discovery, mediation, parent education programs, and other deadlines. Upon receipt of a scheduling order, your attorney's office will forward the order to you and should include a detailed letter explaining the deadlines. You must adhere to the deadlines assigned. It's possible to ask that your case be put on hold, but as the trial date approaches, it may become impossible to keep your case on hold if there is a court imposed scheduling order. A copy of such an order is attached as Exhibit 5.

Dismissal for Want of Prosecution

The court will send your attorney a notice of dismissal for want of prosecution (DWOP) if your case has been dormant for too long. Each court is different, but it is usually after six months that a case will be dismissed if not set for trial or settled. See Exhibit 6.

Response and Counterclaim

The respondent may reply to the petition for divorce with a document called a general denial, an answer, or a response. This document will state the respondent's position regarding each of the claims made in the petition. The respondent may also take this opportunity to initiate a claim in opposition to the petition, such as a claim for custody. This document is called a counterpetition (CP). Do not be worried when the opposing party files a response. This does not automatically mean your case will go to trial or that it will not settle. If the opposing party requests attorney's legal fees, do not have a heart attack. It is a standard request, but rarely do cases get to trial just for a judge to rule on the issue of attorney's legal fees.

When finalizing an uncontested divorce, there is a waiting period of sixty days from the date the original petition was filed before the divorce can be finalized. If your case is uncontested, after your spouse signs a waiver of citation and you have signed your decree of divorce, your attorney can schedule an uncontested hearing Monday through Friday at 8:15 a.m. (or as the court allows). The court appearance generally lasts about an hour, and you will be in front the judge for approximately five minutes. Please wait for your attorney in the courtroom.

Default: When the Opposing Party Does Not Respond

If there is no response (answer) to the original petition in the case, the court will allow you to finalize your divorce by default after the expiration of sixty days. For all practical purposes, however, and in the absence of an agreement between the parties, it is a contested case. The attorneys will have to put on evidence at the final trial. Even if your spouse does not respond, you are still required to put on evidence.

You must file an original answer or counter petition to all petitions. If there is an agreement negotiated as to all disputed matters, finalization can take place on any business day after the expiration of sixty days. If you do not reach an agreement, a trial date can currently be obtained within approximately sixty to ninety days. However, no case can be tried (although there are rare exceptions) until the following has occurred:

1.   At least four months have passed after the filing for the original petition

2.   The parenting class requirements have been fulfilled

3.   A financial disclosure statement has been filed with the court

4.   Mediation has been completed

If there is no agreement negotiated between the parties, then the matter is considered a contest. A pretrial hearing will be scheduled by the court to narrow the issues, at which time the court will probably schedule the case for trial. A case that has gone to mediation and has not settled generally gets scheduled for trial six to nine months after the original petition was served on the respondent. You will probably not go to trial on your first trial date set because the court dockets are overcrowded. Trial usually occurs within eight to fourteen months after filing an OP and service because the courts are overloaded. That is why we encourage arbitration. If the parties cannot settle all the issues by agreement, they can agree to submit to arbitration and set the case for trial before an arbitrator within three to five months. Also, you will have your case heard on the date it is set for arbitration, as opposed to a trial date that most likely will be reset at least once or twice. Arbitration is also much less expensive. Further details on arbitration are discussed in the Alternative Dispute Resolution section.

Chapter 7

ALTERNATIVE DISPUTE RESOLUTION

This was our favorite section of the book to write, because every case should be resolved though alternative dispute resolution. There are several options under alternative dispute resolution. In this section you will learn the benefits of mediation and the difference between mediation, arbitration, and collaborative law. These options are much less expensive than trial. Most lawyers, judges, and mental health professionals agree that is it better to resolve a case by agreement than to have a trial in which a judge decides the outcome. People going through a divorce value the privacy and control that a negotiated agreement offers them. They are more likely to obey a judgment that is based on their agreement than one that has been imposed on them by a judge or jury. Voluntary compliance is important, because enforcement procedures available from the court are usually expensive and sometimes inadequate.

Many Houston family law attorneys might read the above paragraph, and challenge us, stating this is mere lip service because "Allison or Owen are always in trial." That may be true, but the only reason we are in trial and not arbitration is because we failed to settle in mediation and cannot get our opposing counsel to agree to arbitration. More and more attorneys are opting for arbitration as it is so much quicker and less expensive. We have tried to find statistics on mediation but none really exist. We would guess 90 percent of family law cases settle at mediation. If your case does not settle at mediation, you and your attorney need to figure out a way to settle your case, switch into collaborative law, or arbitrate the case before trial. Sometimes, if we are sure the case will not settle at mediation, we go straight to arbitration. The arbitrator will make a binding decision on all the outstanding issues. Each method is described in more detail in the following chapters.

Chapter 8

SETTLEMENT CONFERENCE

The following is the text of Section 6.604 of the Texas Family Code regarding an Informal Settlement Conference between divorcing spouses:

a.   The parties to a suit for dissolution of a marriage may agree to one or more informal settlement conferences. They may also agree that the settlement conferences may be conducted with or without the presence of the parties' attorneys—if they have attorneys.

b.   A written settlement agreement reached at an informal settlement conference is binding on the parties if the agreement:

(1)   provides, in a prominently displayed statement that is in boldfaced type or in capital letters or underlined, that the agreement is not subject to revocation;

(2)   is signed by each party to the agreement; and

(3)   is signed by the parties' attorneys, if any, who is present at the time the agreement is signed.

c.   If a written settlement agreement meets the requirements of Subsection (b), a party is entitled to judgment on the settlement agreement notwithstanding Rule 11, Texas Rules of Civil Procedure, or another rule of law.

d.   If the court finds that the terms of the written informal settlement agreement are just and right, those terms are binding on the court. If the court approves the agreement, the court may set forth the agreement in full or incorporate the agreement by reference in the final decree.

e.   If the court finds that the terms of the written informal settlement agreement are not just and right, the court may request the parties to submit a revised agreement or set the case for a contested hearing.

An informal settlement conference is a meeting between the parties and their lawyers to discuss and resolve all the issues in your case. This is the simplest form of alternative dispute resolution. Informal settlement conferences have several advantages over other forms of alternative dispute resolution. One advantage is that it saves on costs. Other forms of alternative dispute resolution require the participation of third party professionals who must be compensated for their help. In addition, informal settlement conferences can occur at any time or place that is convenient for the parties and their respective attorneys. The scheduling is much more flexible and can accommodate people with difficult schedules. It is also much less expensive. While a divorce is one of the most significant events in a person's life, the world around them continues to move along. The flexibility of the informal settlement process can alleviate the additional stress caused by trying to resolve your divorce. Even if you cannot settle all the issues, it is perfectly acceptable to submit the last remaining issue to the judge or arbitrator. By way of example it might be that you and your spouse resolve all the issues on visitation, rights and duties, and health insurance but cannot settle child support. You can enter into an informal settlement agreement and submit the child support issue to an arbitrator or judge. This will usually take less than two hours to resolve.

If you reach an agreement, the terms of the agreement need to be reduced to writing and signed by you, your spouse, and your respective attorneys. Then, one of the attorneys will be responsible for drafting the final version of that agreement in the form of a judgment, which will then be signed by the parties and filed with the court. The final order in a divorce is called a Decree of Divorce. The final order in a child custody proceeding is called an order in suit affecting parent child relationship or an order in suit to adjudicate parentage. The court must approve your agreement. For example, some Harris County courts will not accept week-on, week-off periods of possession or a final order suit affecting parent-child relationship order with no child support. Your attorney should know each court well enough to avoid these sorts of pitfalls. If the judge rejects your informal settlement agreement, you will have to go back and renegotiate the terms to comply with the court's rules or have a trial.

Many family law cases are resolved through informal settlement conferences. This procedure is most often successful in cases where the parties can communicate amicably and can work well together despite the issues that have led them into litigation. If your case is not a low-conflict case, one of the other methods of alternative dispute resolution described below may be more appropriate.

A key factor in successfully resolving your divorce through an informal settlement conference is preparation. You and your spouse should be prepared to discuss your estate and all issues involving your children, if any, in detail at this conference. You should have access to all of your current financial information, such as bank statements and pay stubs, as well. We have worked with several people who believed that they could report their income and bank balance verbally to their spouse and their spouse's attorney. They are usually shocked when we tell them that we have to have documentation to back up these claims. Having the documents necessary to verify this information will eliminate issues of distrust that can hinder an effective discussion of a resolution. It is common for a spouse to claim that a certain asset is his or her separate property and should not be considered in the divorce. The court requires a very high level of proof to back up claims of separate property. The court actually assumes all property is community property until proven to be separate property.

Another key factor in successfully resolving your divorce is flexibility. You should always know, at the beginning of the process, what it is you want in a final agreement. However, you also need to be able to consider alternatives to your starting proposal. Being flexible about what you are willing to agree to will increase the chances of actually reaching an agreement. We have participated in many informal settlement conferences in which a final agreement seemed impossible, but we were able to reach a settlement because everyone was open to creative solutions.

Chapter 9

MEDIATION: WHAT IS IT AND HOW DOES IT WORK?

Mediation can be set for a half day (four hours), or a full day (eight hours). In this settlement process you, your spouse, and your attorneys meet with a neutral attorney who helps the parties reach a settlement. A mediator cannot force you to settle and will not impose a solution on you but will help you and the opposing party try to find your own solution. You will not be in the same room as your spouse. The parties and their respective attorneys will be in separate rooms with the mediator going back and forth between them. All courts require mediation before a final trial, except in abuse or other extreme circumstances. Many courts require mediation before a temporary orders hearing. Mediation is usually scheduled from 9:00 a.m. to 5:00 p.m. or from 1:00 p.m. to 5:00 p.m. Quite often, it can last until 7:00 p.m. or 8:00 p.m. Please make arrangements for child care if the settlement process runs late.

Who Decides on the Mediator and What Does a Mediator Charge?

The attorneys will choose a mediator to fit your case. If they cannot agree, which is very rare, the court will appoint a mediator. Mediators' fees can be approximately $300 to $700 per party for a half-day mediation and $700 to $1500 per party for a full-day mediation. Mediators require payment by cash, cashier's check or money order. The mediator must be paid *before* the mediation begins. Generally, you are required to pay the mediator directly prior to the start of the mediation. Most do not accept personal checks or credit cards so, as already stated, please make sure you have cash, a cashier's check or a money order. Most mediators also require information that will familiarize them with the issues of your case; your attorney will complete this, but feel free to fax or e-mail your attorney anything you wish the mediator to know. In our office we encourage our clients to add or edit the mediation memo to ensure the mediator is fully informed.

Many cases can be settled by mediation and do not need arbitration or trial at all. One of our favorite mediators is Jane Joseph. Jane Joseph primarily mediates cases in Harris County, Texas and surrounding counties, but every county has good mediators. She mediated nineteen cases in one week in October 2013 and settled all of them. Many days she handles three half-day mediations. She will book mediations in the evening or on weekends. Her office once had a streak of settling forty-three cases straight. We still wonder which attorney was responsible for breaking her settlement streak. She will not tell us.

There are many good mediators in Texas. Your attorney will select a mediator to fit the issues of the case. Tell your attorney if you think your spouse will be more responsive to a male or female, someone older, or who has children the same age as yours. Tell your attorney if your spouse would listen to someone who is more spiritual or more factual. In this way we can match the mediator with the personalities of the parties. You and your spouse are the only two allowed to attend mediation. If you want to bring someone like your CPA, you must get permission from the mediator through your attorney.

Mediators are generally family law attorneys, and in some cases retired family law Judges. Your attorney will find a family law attorney who has a good success rate and handles a lot of family law mediations. We prefer to use an attorney who is board certified in family law or who is a retired judge as a mediator. By hiring a retired judge as your mediator, we can ask him or her, "Based on your many years on the bench, how would you rule on this case?" This should help us to decide if we should settle the case or not. The mediator should discuss the pros and cons of your case and assess your risk of going to trial. Because of the limited number of judges available to hear trials, most courts require the parties and their lawyers to attend mediation. It is often very persuasive to hear from a neutral, experienced professional how they think the judge is likely to rule if the case goes to trial. Although your lawyer may recommend that you accept or reject a particular settlement proposal, the decision to settle is yours. Your lawyer should not make that decision for you. Finally, listen to your lawyer's advice, but recognize that, as with your broker or your certified public accountant, you are the boss.

Even if a case is settled by agreement, your spouse goes to court and you never see the inside of the courthouse, there are certain legal procedures that have to be followed to turn your agreement into a judgment and end your marriage. Your lawyer will see to completing this part of the process, but you have to help. For example, let him or her know what accounts or cars need to be transferred.

Check out the proposed mediator's credentials and qualifications. Also, make sure that the proposed mediator's personality, race, religion, and so on are not a clash with your spouse or parent of your children. All mediations are confidential, and your attorney will never reveal any confidential information. Mediation is a good place to share your outrage or frustration. It is a time to get it all out in the open. Hopefully, you have already shared all of the details with your attorney and you have started to process your emotions so that you can forgive and move on.

Jane Joseph did share with us that people do express their outrage at mediation. At one mediation a man told her, "I am losing my wife; no way I'm giving up my Harley too!" In the very sad category, she reports a young man who was still in high school, attended mediation regarding the oldest of his three children. He got three girls pregnant his junior year of high school. So one wonders (but not really) does that make them triplets if they are all the same age—no! Mediation is an extremely helpful tool in getting your case settled if you are prepared. Make sure you spend time with your attorney, giving them all the information necessary for mediation.

If you reach an agreement, the mediator (or your attorney) will help write out the parameters of the agreement you have reached. This document is called the Mediated Settlement Agreement, MSA for short. All parties will sign the mediated settlement agreement that day. Then, one of the attorneys will be responsible for drafting the final version of that agreement for the parties to sign and file with the court. A signed mediated settlement agreement is *irrevocable*. It is binding and cannot be changed after it's signed. It's important to read the agreement carefully before signing it because you cannot withdraw the agreement and the provisions cannot be renegotiated.

Chapter 10

ARBITRATION

Another method of resolving your case without trial is arbitration. It is similar to a trial and has the same effect as a trial verdict. The case is presented to an independent arbitrator who makes a decision on all outstanding issues. The decision of the arbitrator is binding upon all parties—just as if the case had gone to trial and received a verdict from the judge.

Recently our office had a custody case that would have taken five or six court days, but it was presented to an arbitrator and only required two days. The case was less than five months old when it was arbitrated, and we called eleven witnesses the first day. The attorney's fees were a tenth of what it would have cost to go to trial. In the court it would have taken twelve to fourteen months to get this particular case to trial.

In arbitration the attorneys select an arbitrator, preferably someone who is a board certified family law attorney. In many cases a retired judge is selected as the arbitrator. The cost for arbitration is usually $600 to $1,500 per party per half day. This cost is in addition to your attorney's fees. The difference between arbitration and trial is that trial takes place in the courtroom before an elected or appointed judge. Arbitration takes place at a law office or a law school courtroom and with a paid arbitrator. In arbitration there is no court reporter unless you pay and arrange for one. Again, this process is just as binding as a full blown trial.

The arbitration process is much quicker than a trial. When you go to trial in the court where you are assigned, you are added to the court's trial docket with 30 or more cases set for the same day. On your trial date, you or your attorney will be expected to appear and be ready to proceed to trial. However, the court can reset your trial date. In most cases, the court will reset your trial date several times before your case will actually proceed to trial. This is due to the number of cases on the court's docket. This process is very time-consuming and expensive and you have very little control over when your trial will actually begin. You will also rarely be able to complete the trial from start to finish without interruption. The court still has to conduct day-to-day business and may only be able to give you four or five hours of trial time, even though you are there from 9:00 a.m. until 5:00 p.m., on a particular day. The trial may take place over the course of several days, weeks, or even months.

In contrast, one of the biggest benefits of arbitration is that you are able to schedule the exact date and time that your trial will begin. Typically, the parties and their attorneys will decide beforehand how much time each party will have and how long the arbitration will last. You can schedule it to proceed from start to finish without interruption and to take place in a setting that is less stressful than the courthouse.

Another benefit of arbitration is that it allows the parties and their attorneys to agree to a set of guidelines regarding discovery, presentation of witnesses, and admitting evidence. This flexibility allows you to streamline your case and saves a substantial amount of time and money. This is especially true in the case of expert witnesses, such as CPA's or counselors. These experts need to be paid for their time and need to be booked in advance to be sure that they are available to testify when the time comes. When you proceed through the trial process in court, you normally pay an expert witness to be available for a trial date, only to have that date reset and to have to pay the expert witness again for the next trial setting. If the case proceeds to arbitration, the parties can schedule their expert witnesses to testify at a specific time so that their fees can be paid in advance, and they only need to be paid once for their time.

Even the most highly contested cases can benefit from the arbitration process. In fact, in our experience, these are the cases that benefit the most from going to arbitration. We have been involved in cases that would normally have taken over a year to take to trial and would have cost both sides a tremendous amount in attorney's fees, but because we were able to agree to arbitration the parties saved many thousands of dollars and months of stress.

Once you and your spouse sign an agreement to arbitrate your case, all court intervention is suspended. All decisions will then be made by the arbitrator. After your case is presented to the arbitrator, you will usually receive a verdict within a day or two. A court verdict can take up to a month, or even longer in some cases. The arbitration process is the same as proceeding to trial in that you are presenting your case to a third party to make a decision on the issues. However, through arbitration, you can save yourself and your family a substantial amount of time, money, and stress, and you can begin the healing process much sooner.

Chapter 11

COLLABORATIVE LAW

Collaborative family law was created in the early 1990s, primarily in response to the destructive impact of divorce litigation on divorcing families. It is a nonadversarial process that is focused on moving parties in family law disputes from dispute to resolution with as little financial and emotional damage as possible, while securing an agreement that reflects their true interests.

This is an entirely new model of alternative dispute resolution in Texas. The last fifteen years have seen a growing body of evidence suggesting that more and more married couples, given a safe legal environment within which to work, both want and are uniquely qualified to fashion their own solutions to the issues—without judicial intervention.

Collaborative law seeks to create an environment in which the parties, with the aid of their attorneys, can address the issues as problems to be solved rather than contests to be won. Essential to that process is elimination of the threat, "If you don't agree, we can just let the judge decide." This is accomplished by a written agreement, binding the parties and their attorneys to the proposition that the consequence of failure to reach some solution to all issues presented is the abandonment of the process. Such abandonment means the withdrawal of the attorneys from any further involvement beyond an orderly transition of the matter to new counsel who will, presumably, then prepare the case for trial in the conventional adversarial manner. The resulting atmosphere is one in which the parties and their attorneys have the same conscious incentives to reach a negotiated settlement as well as the same disincentives for failure.

The following is the text of Section 6.603 of the Texas Family Code regarding Collaborative Law:

1.　　Upon written agreement of the parties and their attorneys, a dissolution of marriage proceeding may be conducted under collaborative law procedures.

2.　　Collaborative law is a procedure in which the parties and their attorneys agree in writing to use their best efforts in a good faith attempt to resolve the dissolution of marriage dispute on an agreed-upon basis. The participation of the court is limited to approval of the settlement, making legal pronouncements, and signing the order required by law to effectuate the agreement of the parties as the court determines appropriate. The parties' counsel may not serve as litigation counsel except to ask the court to approve the settlement agreement.

3.　　A collaborative law agreement must include provisions for:

A.　　full and candid exchange of information between the parties and their attorneys as necessary to make a proper evaluation of the case;

B.   suspending court intervention in the dispute while the parties are using collaborative law procedures;

C.   hiring experts, as jointly agreed, to the procedure;

D.   withdrawal of all counsel involved in the collaborative law procedure if the collaborative law procedure does not result in settlement of the dispute; and

E.   other provisions as agreed to by the parties.

If you cannot settle the issues regarding the children on your own or through mediation, the court may appoint (or the parties can agree on) an amicus attorney to represent the children. Other options are that the parties may order a mental health evaluation or a social study. If a parent has been abusing drugs or alcohol, the court may order an alcohol/drug evaluation or testing. Each of these processes is described in the following chapters.

Chapter 12

DISCOVERY REQUESTS

One of the most expensive and time-consuming parts of the trial process is discovery. This stage is also one of the most important parts of the trial process. At this stage of the case you need to gather all of the evidence you will need to present as well as information about any witnesses that you have so you can provide it to the opposing side in a timely manner. The Rules of Civil Procedure state that you cannot use any evidence or witnesses that were not provided properly during discovery.

Each spouse is entitled to information from the other about the case. The legal procedures for obtaining that information are called discovery. Discovery may be a simple, speedy process or one consuming a great deal of time, energy, and money. Requests for disclosures, interrogatories, requests for production of documents and requests for admissions are several tools used to gather information from the other party. Discovery is governed by rules regarding the manner and time of filing responses. Attorneys can agree to certain deadlines for responding to discovery, but if no agreement can be reached, you must comply with the discovery deadlines provided by the Texas Rules of Civil Procedure. If you cannot respond on time, you must let your attorney's office know immediately as it will be necessary to discuss the best way to handle the situation. There are serious consequences to not responding to discovery requests within thirty days. You can be fined. The opposing party could file a motion to compel and you could be responsible for the attorney fees. Discovery may also be conducted informally. It is often more efficient and less expensive for lawyers to informally exchange documents and information than to do formal discovery through the written requests listed above. Responding to formal requests for discovery is very time consuming and expensive and can cause spouses to incur a substantial amount of attorneys fees creating these formal responses. If you exchange the documents informally, you can avoid incurring the cost of preparing these formal responses.

Throughout your case, your attorney will request that you supply documents needed to prove your case as well as to respond to requests made by the other party. While the requests may be time-consuming, they are absolutely necessary. Delay in sending documents will increase complications in your case significantly, so please do respond promptly. It can also make the cost of your attorney's fees double.

Requests for Disclosures

These requests are utilized to notify the court and the parties of all the basic facts pertaining to the case including: the basic issues in dispute, the identity of fact and expert witnesses, their names and addresses, the scope of their knowledge, and likely testimony. This discovery requires a response, in writing, thirty days from the date the other party serves the request. If, in response to this discovery, the opposing party fails to divulge the name, address, and telephone number of an expert witness and the nature of his or her testimony, your attorney can request that the judge strike that witness from testifying.

Interrogatories

Interrogatories are written questions sent by one party to the other inquiring as to any matter that relates to the case. You will have thirty days from the date of receipt to answer all of the questions. You must answer almost anything that is asked even if you don't think it is relevant. These answers will have the same effect as testimony in open court so you must take them seriously. You must give a formal response to *every* question. You will have to swear to the truthfulness of the answers and your answers must be signed by you in front of a notary public.

Request for Production of Documents

This discovery tool allows your attorney to request copies of documents that will assist us in determining: the value of the estate, the earning power of the other party, and other important information. The response must be provided within thirty days of the receipt of the request. If a document is requested but is not provided in the response, usually the responding party may not introduce the document into evidence at the time of trial.

Request for Admissions

Admissions require a party to admit or deny the truthfulness of specific statements. If the responses are not answered and filed within thirty days of their receipt, the court may deem all the statements admitted as true. These are rarely used in family law cases.

All discovery is used as a tool in preparing the case for trial. Essential information can be obtained from the opposing party, banks, or financial institutions that will assist in preparing the case for settlement or trial.

Discovery is extremely important, and your attorney needs your full cooperation. If you have *any* questions, contact your attorney's office immediately.

Your spouse's attorney will require current statements regarding your checking and savings accounts, retirement, brokerage accounts, and credit card statements. You do not have to wait for a request to be filed to start gathering your documents. Some documents may require extensive time to gather, so start gathering documents at the beginning of the process. It is extremely smart, although not necessary, to gather the document listed in chapter 3 before you file or even visit your attorney.

Chapter 13

DEPOSITION

In a deposition, the spouses, the experts, and other parties (e.g., a girlfriend or counselor) may be required to answer questions under oath in a lawyer's office while a court reporter takes down all questions and answers. The court reporter will prepare a transcript of the testimony.

In its simplest form, a deposition is the oral testimony of a witness or a party, taken under oath, before the commencement of a trial. The attorney can ask almost any questions of you or any other witness. The questions asked only need to be reasonably calculated to lead to information that is relevant to the case or to discovering relevant facts. The rules by which Texas courts operate allow either side in a lawsuit to take a deposition of the other side or of any witness within 150 miles of the courthouse. A witness who lives outside of the 150-mile range can still be deposed, but the deposition will have to take place in the witness's city of residence and will cost much more. A deposition may be taken in your attorney's office, the opposing attorney's office, or another place that is mutually agreed upon. A judge will not be present. However, what you say will be recorded by shorthand, court reporter, audio and/or videotape. Although your attorney will be present, it is *your* deposition. The strength of *your* case will depend on how you answer the questions, your attitude, your truthfulness, and your appearance!

Why is your deposition being taken? That's simple—the opposing side wants to "pick your brain." They want to find out what facts you know regarding this lawsuit, and they want to pin you down to a specific story. If you answer a question one way during the deposition and another way during the trial, your honesty is questioned. To avoid such difficulties, it's helpful to remember the following:

1.   Take your time answering questions; speak slowly and clearly.

2.   If you don't understand a question, ask the attorney to restate the question or say "I do not understand the question."

3.   Answer the question you are asked and then *stop* talking. Never try to explain your answer. If you can answer yes or no, do so and *stop*.

4.   Relax and listen calmly. The opposing attorney may try to make you angry in hopes that you will say something you will regret later (like at trial!).

5.   Stick to the *basic* facts and testify only to that which you *personally* know. This means don't speculate, don't give your opinion, and don't estimate things like time, speed, or distance unless you have a good reason for knowing such matters.

6.   Do believe your attorney when she says tell the truth. In a lawsuit, the truth is never as damaging as a lie!

7.   While you may think a particular question or a possible
        answer to a question is cute or funny, it's doubtful that you
        think your lawsuit is funny. *Do* treat the whole deposition
        seriously.

8.   Answer the questions to the best of your ability. It is not
        necessary to memorize information in advance.

9.   If you honestly don't know the answer to a question then
        admit it with the simple response, "I don't know."

10.   Be on guard. Remember, the *other* attorney is your "legal
        enemy." *Do not* let his or her friendly manner cause you to
        drop your guard or become chatty. A deposition is *not* a
        social event. Don't be chummy—either with the opponents
        or their attorneys—before, during, or after the deposition.
        On the other hand, your attorney will not permit you to be
        intimidated at deposition.

11.   Don't socialize with the Court Reporter. They are likely to
        share what you told them with the other party's attorney.

12.   Although attorneys are allowed to object during the
        deposition to certain questions, these objections are
        extremely limited, and you must answer the majority, if not
        all, of the questions.

13.   Don't be smart or answer with a response like "you
        have asked me that three times already." Just answer the
        question.

The first opportunity that the opposing attorney has to see you usually comes at the deposition. He or she will use the occasion to try to size

up both you and your case. Therefore, it is important that you make a good impression; you should prepare as if you were going to trial. Use your common sense, and that means *you should:* be neat; wear a suit. Please treat all persons in the deposition room with respect.

Chapter 14

TRIAL AND EXHIBITS

In the unfortunate event that your case does not settle, you will need to be present at the trial setting. Please call your attorney's office to confirm the date, time, and location. It's most likely that your case will not be heard by the judge on that day. Family law cases are assigned to a two-week trial docket and may be called at any time during that two-week period. There is a high likelihood that your case will not be reached during the first two week period that your case is on the trial docket. Our office has tried a lot of cases, and we have begun trial twice on the first trial setting. One was in Galveston County around 1985 and the other in Harris County. There are normally about thirty other cases set for final trial on the same day. Your case could be called on the first trial setting or within two weeks, so you must be prepared, and your attorney must subpoena all witnesses to each trial setting. The court will hear the oldest cases first. If the court does not have time to hear your case, it will be reset in approximately four to twelve weeks. Your attorney has no control over the court or when your case will be heard. It is just as hard on counsel as it is on you. Please understand that we will do everything in our power to resolve your case as quickly as possible. If mediation is unsuccessful, please do not give up on trying to settle your case. We encourage you to keep thinking of ways to resolve your case before going to trial.

After discovery is complete, and if you are unable to settle all issues in a case, you must present your case to a judge or jury. That is a trial. The purpose of a trial is to present your case, both the law and the facts, in the most favorable light possible. This is done in a courtroom, and you have a specific role in your case's presentation. Going through a trial in a custody case or a divorce is one of the worst experiences that a person can have. The good news, however, is that it ends. Once the trial is over, most of my clients feel like the weight of the world has been lifted off of their shoulders. This section will provide some information on how a case proceeds through the process of trial.

To prepare for a final trial or a temporary orders hearing you will need to present evidence in the form of exhibits, witnesses, your testimony, and perhaps a social study or mental health evaluation. It is your responsibility to bring any pertinent documents to your attorney's attention. There is a list of possible exhibits to help jog your memory, included below, but there can be many more than those listed.

Docket Call

In most Texas counties, your case is assigned a trial date. This is the date on which your case is called on the court's docket. Trials rarely start on that date. If the court does not have time to hear your case, it will be assigned a new trial date, usually thirty days later. In most large counties, including Harris, Galveston, and Ft. Bend, cases almost never proceed to trial on the first trial date that's set.

Exhibits

Frequently, words alone are not enough to get the point across. Exhibits are used to show the judge or jury the evidence. In property cases, there must first be a list of all property to be divided. In addition, your attorney must have the original or a copy of the following:

1.   Proof of ownership. All titles, mortgage, and notes showing ownership of real or personal property.

2.   Accounts with financial institutions. Statements from financial institutions reflecting checking accounts, savings accounts, stocks, bonds, certificates of deposits, money market accounts, and so forth.

3.   Life insurance. All documents reflecting life insurance coverage and the cash value.

4.   Income. Documents reflecting your income, including wage statements, income tax returns, interest, and rental income statements, and 1099 forms.

5.   Debts. A copy of all statements from financial institutions (promissory notes, etc.) showing monies owed to an individual or organization.

6.   A list of furniture and personal property reflecting garage sale prices.

In custody cases, provide your attorney with documentation that shows your involvement with your child, including, but not limited to any of the following:

1.   Photographs showing you with your child, your home, your spouse's home, and anything else you can think of.

2.   School records such as report cards (especially if your spouse has had temporary custody and your child's grades and conduct have declined, or if you have had temporary custody and the grades and conduct have improved). Other

school records will show attendance and even a parent's involvement.

3. Audiotapes of conversations between you and someone else, especially the other party. Texas is one of the states where some tape-recorded telephone conversations are admissible. Such conversations are admissible in court if the proper predicate is laid. You must be one of the parties to the conversation. You must record the date and time of each call. ***Recording conversations between other people who are not aware of such recording (including your spouse and child) may be illegal.*** Bear in mind that listening to hours of tapes is not a good use of your attorney's time (or his fees to you), so transcribe the tapes, and make a copy for the opposing attorney and the amicus attorney. Sometimes audiotapes can reveal how bitter, hateful, and angry the other parent really is, and that any testimony of the parent displaying kindness and lack of bitterness is phony. This will be explained in more detail in a later chapter.

Parents need to be very careful about recording conversations without a person's knowledge. Under Texas law at the time that this book was written, a person can record a conversation that they are a party to without notifying the other person. However, this Texas law may not apply to recording a conversation where the other person is in another state or traveling across state lines. In addition, other laws will apply to intercepting communications that are not sent to you, such as e-mails or text messages. Please make sure you consult with your attorney before you start recording conversations or making copies of other communications without a person's knowledge. Make sure you are not violating any state or federal statutes.

If a person violates one of the various state or federal statutes on wiretapping or intercepting communications, they can be subject to criminal penalties as well as civil penalties with statutory damages. Additionally, they can be sued for invasion of privacy or other civil claims as well.

4. Videotapes of you and your child or children doing things together or of property in dispute. One of the best video tapes we have seen is a dad taking his daughter fishing. The close bond and mutual love was easy to see. It spoke volumes to the jury. At trial, "A Day in the Life" tapes are beneficial.

5. Letters from the other parent showing bitterness and any attempt to damage the bond between you and your children.

6. Birthday, Valentine's Day, Mother's and Father's Day cards to you in which the other parent admits what a good person and/or parent you are; letters and cards from the children showing how much the child loves you and what a close bond you have with each other.

7. Medical records can also be helpful, especially if they show how a child was neglected while in the custody of the other parent. These can be admitted into evidence by means of a business record affidavit. This eliminates the need to have a doctor testify at trial. A physician can testify as to whether or not a child has any special needs.

8. Awards to you, such as coaching little league sports or serving as den leader in Boy Scouts or Girl Scouts.

9.   Checks, financial receipts, and so on showing that the other parent is not only wasting money, but that money is the other parent's priority rather than the child or children. This includes checks to liquor stores and payments for luxury items.

10.   Tax returns showing the other parent's income or that he or she was dishonest with the IRS.

11.   Telephone records showing attempts by you to talk with the children and vice versa. Also, records showing that you encouraged the children to call their grandparents on a regular basis.

12.   Religious documents showing that you took the child or children to church or synagogue and achieved certain plateaus within your faith.

13.   Clothing—if the other parent dresses the child in filthy or torn clothes.

14.   Inappropriate toys, games, books, or video games the other parent has given the child.

15.   You need to show the jury a large color photograph, at least eight inches by ten inches, of each child. Potential jurors will lean forward in their chairs to obtain a good look and therefore listen very closely to the evidence. Seeing a photograph makes the jury members want to pay attention and make the right decision. They will recognize that the child's life is in their hands.

16.   Judgments or criminal convictions pertaining to the other
        parent, including driving records.

17.   Surveillance tapes. If your spouse was having an affair
        or at the bars drinking a lot, we may be able to subpoena
        surveillance tapes.

Chapter 15

WITNESSES

P lease go through all of the important criteria set forth above and think of: people who have personal knowledge of either your good qualities or your spouse's bad qualities (if you are involved in custody litigation); people with personal knowledge regarding all such factors as are pertinent to the issues of your case. You want to think about what you are trying to prove and who has the knowledge to assist you. They may only know of a specific incident or may know a great deal about you, your spouse, the children, or the property involved. A witness questionnaire is attached. Such people include

1.   your family;

2.   neighbors and former neighbors;

3.   coworkers;

4.   your employees and/or employers;

5.   school teachers of the child;

6.   day care workers;

7.   coaches and scout leaders;

8.   church friends and clergymen;

9.   physicians;

10.   fellow charity workers;

11.   your certified public accountant;

12.   real estate agents; and

13.   your financial advisor or banker.

Hiring an investigator to see what your spouse is doing can be very important, especially to determine how your spouse is spending his or her time. The testimony of such an investigator is important because it will be based on personal knowledge.

Make a list of possible witnesses, including their addresses and telephone numbers. Give this to your attorney along with specific details about each witness's testimony so questions can be prepared accordingly. Your attorney will provide you with a witness questionnaire for the witness to complete but it is general in nature. It can be in digital or hard copy format. We suggest you have as many people who fit in the list above fill out a witness questionnaire or write a narrative describing his or her knowledge.

The Texas Rules of Civil Procedure require that each party disclose specific information about each witness, including address, telephone number, and a brief statement of his or her relation to the case. If this information is not provided, the witness will not be permitted to testify. We once represented a parent in a highly contested custody case, and the most important witness was almost prevented from testifying because her phone number was not provided in discovery.

Chapter 16

JURY SELECTION

In this book we have chosen not to spend much time on a jury trial because less than 0.5 percent of the cases are decided by a jury. If your case is going to be decided by a jury, make an appointment with your attorney to go through the process in much more detail. This section only applies if you or the other party has requested a jury trial.

Either party to a divorce has the right to pay a jury fee and have a jury decide his or her case. While a jury trial is more expensive, it is an option that is available to you and should be discussed with your attorney. The fee to request a jury trial in Texas is only $35.00, but it would double the amount of your attorney's fees.

It is critical to exclude potential jurors that are biased against you. In an early stage of the trial, called voir dire, specific questions will be asked of potential jurors by counsel for both parties in an attempt to weed out those who admit to bias. The attorneys will explain that feelings are neither right nor wrong, they just exist. This will be done to get a potential juror to admit that bias can be natural, and it is not necessarily wrong to feel a certain way. Each potential juror, rather than the jury panel as a group, will be asked if he or she feels that children should be raised by their mothers or fathers after a divorce, and whether gender would influence his or her thinking and possibly their verdict.

Most custody cases last two to three days. If your case is decided by a jury, it will likely take four to five days.

Chapter 17

TRIAL TESTIMONY

One of the most important parts of the trial will be your testimony before the court. This is your opportunity to tell your side of the case and show the court who you are and why you should be able to get what you are asking for. When you are in the courtroom, your demeanor, tone, attitude, and appearance are on display, and all will play a role in how you are perceived. You will not only be judged by the words that come out of your mouth, but also by your body language and demeanor while in court. Below are some guidelines to follow to help ensure that you present yourself well.

Rules Regarding Trial and Your Trial Testimony

1. Be aware of your behavior at all times. Sit in the spectator area unless otherwise directed.

2. Dress appropriately.

3. Be punctual. Be attentive to the proceedings.

4. Advise your attorney of any medication you need to take.

5.   Do not read in the courtroom while court is in session.

6.   Make sure your cell phones or mobile devices are turned off.

7.   Do not smoke, chew gum, eat, or drink in the courtroom.

8.   Do not take any weapons to the courthouse area. Most courthouses have a metal detector you must go through.

9.   Rise when responding to the court or when the judge enters the courtroom. Do not address the judge directly, only answer the judge's question.

10.   Keep the volume of your voice loud enough so the court reporter can record your testimony.

11.   Other than saying hello, do not talk with opposing counsel.

12.   Always use a pleasant tone of voice. Do not use profanity or vulgar language under any circumstances. If you are asked a question to which the answer contains profanity, spell the words instead of pronouncing them. Be wary of making statements or comments in the restrooms or other places because they may be overheard. If you talk to one of the witnesses, that witness could be excluded from testifying. If he or she has already testified, that testimony could be stricken from the record.

13.   Always be respectful. Be careful of your body language both on and off the witness stand. Once you park your car, assume everything you do is being observed.

14.   When talking with your attorney, attempt to assure the privacy of the conservation.

15.   During the trial do not distract your attorney. Communicate with him or her in writing. Do not talk in court unless you are on the witness stand.

16.   Do not take notes with you to the witness stand without the permission of your attorney. Remove all notes from the courtroom each day.

17.   Do not make objections to the wording of the witness oath.

18.   At the request of either party, the witnesses on both sides may be required to remain outside of the courtroom while the other witnesses are testifying. If this requirement is imposed, do not violate it.

19.   Do not arrange for your boyfriend or girlfriend or minor children to attend the trial as spectators.

20.   During the trial do not leave the courtroom without permission from your attorney.

21.   Do not be suspicious of the attorney and judge conducting in-chambers conferences. It is normal.

22.   During your testimony, always be truthful.

23.   Listen to the questions you are asked and make sure you understand them before answering. Provide only the information which answers the question. Do not speculate or guess at an answer. Do not volunteer information.

24. Stay focused. Do not be distracted by people entering the courtroom or by the activity of the clerks.

25. Do not lose your temper. Remain polite and calm during your testimony. Do not argue with opposing counsel.

26. Address all counsel formally and not by first names.

27. Do not try to rush your answer. If an attorney stands up, stop your answer in midsentence if necessary. Wait patiently for objections to be ruled upon. If the judge says overruled, please answer. Otherwise, wait for the next question.

28. Avoid the use of words such as "never" and "always." Don't say, "To tell you the truth," or "To be honest with you," under any circumstances.

You will be a witness. If you have testified in prior hearings or given deposition testimony, you already have some understanding of the dos and don'ts of testifying. But if this is your first experience, you should consider the following suggestions. The overriding consideration in your testimony is to be truthful. Irrespective of the courtroom dramas on television, the worst thing you can do is lie under oath. If it is proven by the opposing side that you've lied, your credibility is destroyed. This is particularly true in a bench trial, where the trier of facts is a judge, who will probably be far less tolerant of lying than a jury might be. Since your communications with your attorney enjoy absolute privilege, any damaging information should be revealed to your attorney long before the start of a trial. In that way, a strategy for how that information is to be presented or dealt with will have been addressed by the time you are giving testimony.

It is the attorney's job, not the task of the witness, to get the evidence before the court. The witness's job is to listen to the question and answer only the question that is asked. Since you are going to be held to your answers, be sure that you understand the questions before you reply to them. Do not guess. If the question contains a word you do not understand, do not hesitate to ask the attorney to state the question in such a way that you do understand it.

Further, you are not to volunteer information. If you feel the answer is inadequate, your attorney will follow up with other clarifying questions. Do not speculate while answering questions. If you do not know an answer, say so. If the attorney has asked you to answer a question yes or no, be sure that every assumption or statement in the question is accurate before responding yes; otherwise the answer should be no. You may pause a reasonable amount of time to formulate an answer, but lengthy pauses sometimes give the appearance of evading the truth. You should attempt to be as responsive as possible to avoid this impression. This can generally be accomplished by being as attentive as possible and staying focused. Do not get distracted by trying to figure out what objectives the opposing attorney is trying to achieve.

Your tone of voice should always be pleasant, polite, and calm, and your demeanor and mannerisms should appear as relaxed as possible. The volume of your voice should be sufficiently loud so that everyone can hear without straining. Anger does not project well in a courtroom even when it is totally justified, and you are to avoid loss of temper for any reason. You should not be argumentative with the opposing counsel or "take him on." He or she is experienced, you are not, and generally you will come out a loser.

If you are being asked questions by one counsel, and during that questioning or immediately after the question, the other attorney rises or says "objection," stop talking immediately, as the attorney wants to address the court and is requesting a ruling. Do not rush to answer because you think it is helpful to your cause. Patiently wait for the objection to be lodged and for the court to rule. In that regard, if the opposing attorney's objection is based on "nonresponsive" and the court sustains the objection, it means you are volunteering and answering more than the question asked. An example is,

"Please state your name." Assume the answer given is, "My name is Sally Sue Brown, and I was born in San Antonio, Texas, in 1955." The answer is nonresponsive after "Brown," since no one asked where you were born or the year in which you were born.

When you take the stand to testify, do not take any documents or notes with you other than those that your attorney has directed you to have. If you testify from a document, the opposing counsel is entitled to examine that document. Further, if your attorney, not opposing attorney, hands you a document with which you are familiar and asks you to identify the document, do so promptly without reading every line of every page, as though you had never seen the document before. If opposing counsel tenders you a document, look at it sufficiently to be certain it is a document with which you are familiar and then promptly identify it. That does not mean that you should identify a document with which you have no familiarity or that may have been altered. What you want to avoid is an unreasonable and unnecessary long delay in time in identifying familiar documents.

When the petitioner's attorney concludes the presentation of the petition's evidence, the petitioner will rest. Many times the court will allow opposing counsel to call one of his witness during our presentation of your case as an accommodation to the witness. This is normal.

Chapter 18

THE COURTROOM

The Courthouse Complex

As mentioned above, the scrutiny of your conduct and behavior, together with that of your attorney, starts in the parking lots surrounding the courthouse. It is there that you may first be observed by potential jurors, court personnel, prospective witnesses, or anyone else who may have an impact on the final result of your trial. Therefore, from the time of your arrival at the courthouse complex, you must be conscious of how others may perceive you or your behavior.

Go to the courthouse the week before your trail starts to find the courtroom and get comfortable.

The Courtroom

You may have already appeared in a courtroom for some preliminary hearings. If you have, you know that a courtroom looks similar to what you have seen on television. The judge is at the front of the courtroom, elevated above everyone so he can see everything from his bench. There is a place for the court personnel, generally a clerk or two, a bailiff, and a court reporter. There is a special place for the witness to sit, generally referred to as the witness stand. There is a jury box with twelve seats and it is usually located to one side so the jurors can observe everything that goes on in the courtroom.

As you come into the courtroom, you will probably walk into the spectator area. There is a gate through which you and your attorney will pass at the appropriate time that leads to the counsel table(s) before the judge's bench. Your attorney will inform you as to when you are to enter and where you are to sit. During all other times that your trial is not in session, except for brief breaks, you will sit in the spectator's section.

Before any trial starts you need to know the location of the rest rooms, water fountains, and cafeteria. There are also areas that the public is forbidden to enter, such as the areas behind the court's clerks.

Decorum in the Courtroom

If you have any doubts about your dress or behavior, check with your attorney's office. Your clothing should be appropriate and relatively bland (the June and Ward Cleaver model). In other words, there should be nothing ostentatious or flashy. You cannot go wrong if, as you leave the house, you get a negative answer to the question, "Would my mother be embarrassed if I took her to church dressed as I am?"

Women should avoid flashy jewelry, bright-colored nail polish, tight clothing, short skirts, low-cut blouses or dresses, unkempt hair, and the like. Men should avoid flashy jewelry, an unshaven look (unless they normally have facial hair), unkempt hair, shirts unbuttoned significantly below the neckline with a show of gold chains or jewelry, and wearing hats in the courtroom. No one can go wrong wearing an understated suit to court.

Any lapel pins suggesting your position on provocative political, religious, or social issues should be removed to avoid evoking any adverse response. You will not wear dark glasses in the courtroom unless ordered to by a doctor. There is no gum chewing or eating in the courtroom. Many courthouses currently are no smoking facilities or have specified smoking areas. These policies must be scrupulously followed. You must turn your cellular telephone *off*.

General Behavior

Always be punctual for court. Be sure you know the exact time you are supposed to be in the courtroom. Be sure to give yourself sufficient time to deal with any traffic congestion, finding a parking place, walking from the parking place to the courthouse, going through the security system, waiting for an elevator, and getting to the courtroom. In some major metropolitan areas there can be a considerable lapse of time between arriving in the courthouse complex and getting into the courtroom, depending upon the time of day or the day of the week. Ask a staff member for some assistance in gauging your time so that you can be punctual.

At all times be attentive to the proceedings. You will not be attending your trial in a vacuum. Before trial, you will have read your deposition to be certain you are familiar with your prior testimony. You will have read and refreshed your recollection as to the answers you previously gave in response to the interrogatories that have been asked of you. You may have read any prior testimony in earlier hearings. You will have reviewed critical documents. You will have refamiliarized yourself with your inventory and updated it for any changes. You should be prepared for the questions your attorney will ask you as well as for potential questions the opposing party's attorney might ask you. You will have talked with your attorney about the theme of your case or your theory of recovery, with an awareness of the advantages of your case and anticipated pitfalls that may exist. You will have been completely truthful with your attorney, and he or she will have offered you guidance on how to handle various issues. So as you approach trial, you will have an understanding of the issues and evidence anticipated. An informed client who pays attention to the proceedings can be a help as opposed to a hindrance to his or her attorney.

Be very careful of your body language, both while court is in session and when it is not, whether you are testifying or sitting at counsel table. Body language sometimes speaks louder than words, and it can be particularly significant to an experienced judge in a bench trial. Dramatic gestures, grimaces, vigorous and even subtle shakes and nods of the head, furious writing, drumming on the table with pen, pencils or fingers, mouthing unspoken words to the opposite side of the table, mouthing unspoken words to a witness while he or she is testifying, passing or throwing notes to the opposite side of the counsel table, whispering statements to your attorney in such a loud voice that the opposite side, the court, or court personnel can hear what you are saying, clicking of ball point pens, jingling change, or use of profanity are all types of body language and behavior to avoid.

If it is necessary for you to take any medication during the course of your trial, you need to alert your attorney, either directly or through a staff member, so arrangements can be made to ensure you have an appropriate opportunity to do so. If you are on any particular medication during your trial, your attorney must have that information before trial starts.

It is acceptable to bring a book or magazine to keep you occupied during court breaks, recesses, or other interruptions during the trial. However, reading these items is generally not permitted in the courtroom while court is in session.

As stated previously, make sure your telephone is off while you are in the courtroom.

It is totally unacceptable to bring any type of weapon to the court-room. Most courthouses now have electronic security systems that you must go through to gain admittance to the courthouse. We have had three cases where a party or a witness was arrested on their way into the Courthouse on the day of trial because they were in possession of a weapon.

Chapter 19

COURT RULES

When You Rise

Rising momentarily when a judge enters the courtroom is a recognized sign of respect. Frequently as a judge enters the courtroom, a bailiff will say something to the effect of "All rise! The Judicial District Court is now in session, the Honorable John Doe, presiding." In such an event, of course, you rise and remain standing until the judge directs that all be seated.

You will observe that attorneys are expected to rise when addressing the judge. Since you are never to address the judge directly, unless the judge has directed a matter to you that calls for a response, you may stand when addressing the court (i.e. judge) but it is not imperative. Certainly standing to address the court will show proper respect, but many times a judge will suggest that a party remain seated. If that is the case, then do so.

Conversing with Others

In the event the judge asks a question directly to you, you are to respond in a respectful manner, truthfully, and in a voice loud enough to be heard.

Other than for social amenities you should not engage in conversation with opposing counsel or the opposing party in the courtroom, during breaks or otherwise, without the presence of your attorney and your attorney's permission. That does not mean to say you must engage in social amenities, but they are permissible. In any event, when you are conversing with anyone in the courtroom or the courthouse complex, always use a pleasant tone of voice, and be absolutely certain to use appropriate language. One should be particularly wary of making statements in rest rooms where you may be overheard by somone whom you did not know was there. Harsh, angry, hostile comments containing expletives or revealing statements have no place in the courtroom or where they can be easily overheard by a judge, potential witness, juror, opposing counsel or staff, or court personnel. There is a tremendous risk that the conversation will be reported to others, resulting in damage to your case.

Communicating with Your Attorney

If court is not in session and you need to talk with your attorney, advise him or her that you need to do so and converse in a manner that will assure the privacy of the conversation.

If your attorney is engaged in a trial, you simply cannot communicate with him or her verbally. It is impossible for an attorney to follow the evidence and court's rulings and simultaneously talk or listen effectively to a client. You should have a note pad and pen in front of you at all times during the trial, and make notes about matters that you need to discuss with your attorney at the appropriate time. If you have something to point out relating to the ongoing testimony, write a note and very discretely pass it to your attorney for disposition as he or she sees fit. If your attorney chooses at that moment not to use your written questions, information, or suggestion, wait until there is a recess to discuss the matter.

Do not tap your attorney to get his attention. Do not start whispering to him about the witness, the testimony, or a question to be asked. Attorneys need to keep their undivided attention on the matters before them, and you should not interfere with that concentration. However, that does not mean that a helpful note placed before him or her cannot be useful and constructive.

At the conclusion of the day's testimony, be sure that all notes you and your attorney have exchanged are in either your possession or that of your attorney. Do not leave them on the counsel table or put them in the courtroom wastebasket for possible pilfering and review by the opposition.

Evidence and Witnesses

Texas law is very specific about procedures for admitting evidence at trial and what witnesses can and cannot testify about. It is normal for attorneys to object to the opposing party's evidence and questions for witnesses. Many of the objections will sound very accusatory and may seem harsh, but they are normally expressed in legal terms of art that have very specific meaning. The Texas Rules of Civil Procedure are the rules that apply generally to a case that proceeds in all Texas courts. The provisions of the Texas Family Code apply to issues in family law cases. There are additional statutes that may apply to your case as well, such as those found in the Texas Rules of Evidence. Typically, each court has a set of local rules that apply in that court and they should always be followed as well.

After you have reviewed these rules and the attachments, if you have any questions, concerns, or fears, you should discuss them with your attorney or one of the staff members. Alternatively, you can observe the courtroom and the judge before whom your case is going to be tried during a trial similar to yours. You may find that experience helpful in getting a clear insight as to what to expect during your own trial. Please coordinate with the legal assistant so you don't waste a trip to the courthouse if the judge is on a holiday. You can also go to a trial to view opposing counsel in action. It may be helpful to see how the opposing counsel conducts himself or herself and to view the cross-examination of the opposing party.

Chapter 20

PRELIMINARY TRIAL MATTERS

Most preliminary or pretrial matters are heard before the trial of the case on the merits. However, upon occasion there are preliminary issues that have to be resolved on the first day of trial and before the commencement of trial, such as the ruling upon a law issue, the failure of a witness under subpoena to appear, the exchange of some documentary information, or the like. These matters are generally handled by the attorneys and judge, and your participation is limited except perhaps for sitting at counsel table, awaiting the outcome.

Swearing in the Witnesses

At the beginning of the trial proceeding, commonly the court will ask all witnesses to rise, raise their right hand, and take the witness oath. The court endeavors to try to have all the subpoenaed witnesses sworn in at one time to avoid having to repeat the swearing in process with each witness. Since you will be a witness, you will rise, raise your hand, and take the oath at that time.

The oath that will be administered will probably be: "Do you solemnly swear (or affirm) that the testimony you are about to give in the case pending before this court will be the truth, the whole truth, and nothing but the truth, so help you God?" If for any religious or moral reason you have any compunction about taking this oath, you need to address the problem with your attorney or a staff member before you get to court.

Invoking the Rule

At one point in the trial, but generally before the first witness testifies, either attorney may announce to the court that he or she is requesting that "the rule be invoked." The judge will then instruct all witnesses, except the parties, to leave the courtroom, stand outside the hearing of any of the proceedings, and not discuss their testimony with anyone except the attorneys involved. The failure of a witness to comply with the court's instructions can result in that witness being held in contempt of court, fined, and/ or unable to testify.

Once the rule has been invoked, you must be certain to abide by the rule as well. You are not to discuss your testimony or the testimony of any other witnesses with any other person who may testify. You are not free to discuss testimony after that particular witness has testified, as the rule endures throughout the trial of the case. If you violate the rule, valuable testimony for your case may be excluded during the trial.

Attendance of Observers, Family, or Friends

A trial is a public hearing and, although spectators are allowed, generally there are very few public observers during a divorce trial. As a consequence, other than the court personnel, attorneys, and parties to the divorce action, you will probably not have many people listening to your case. This is particularly true if your case runs into the afternoon or lasts more than one day. If you desire having a family member, friend, or member of a support group present, the person you select should not be a potential witness, since witnesses are generally required to wait outside the courtroom. Further, many times when an attorney sees a friend of the opposing party, he will ask the judge to swear the person in for the sole purpose of expelling the friend from the courtroom during the trial. On the other hand, attorneys sometimes agree that friends or supporters may remain in the courtroom if they are not witnesses. By all means avoid asking your lover (significant other) to be in the courtroom for the trial of your divorce case. Also, do not have your minor children accompany you to any court hearings.

Leaving the Courtroom

If the court is not in session, you may leave and return at will. You may also leave and return if the court is in session on a matter unrelated to yours, such as another case, and you are in the spectator section. If you do leave, do so quietly so as not to disturb or interrupt the proceedings. Remember that you cannot leave the courtroom during the trial of your case without permission. Normally, courts take breaks during the conduct of a trial, at which time you are free to leave and return to the courtroom at will. If you have a crisis that necessitates your leaving the courtroom, pass a note to your attorney indicating that need, and he or she will seek permission from the court to enable you to leave. If this is a critical issue with you, obtain guidance on this matter from your attorney before the trial.

Length of the Trial

The length of a trial varies from case to case and court to court. Obviously one of the factors is the complexity of issues and evidence involved. Since courts conduct ancillary (interim) hearings and have other professional and administrative duties and responsibilities, all of which take considerable time, another factor is how the court conducts its business. If time is important to you, consult with your attorney or the law office staff about the probable length of your case.

In-Chambers Conferences

Upon occasion, the judge requests that both attorneys confer with him or her in chambers, which many clients view with great suspicion. If the judge makes such a request, your attorney has no alternative but to join opposing counsel and the judge—to do otherwise would be offensive and against your interests. What usually transpires during an in-chambers conference is an effort by the court to streamline the case, to see if the court can do anything to expedite the case and to resolve scheduling matters that may arise due to the length of the case. The court will endeavor, in this relatively informal atmosphere, to become familiar with the issues, determine how many witnesses may be involved, obtain the attorneys' estimate of time for the trial of the case, explore any possibility of settlement or stipulations (agreements) of the parties, make sure that all exhibits have been marked and/or exchanged, and ascertain if there are any significant legal issues. If done properly, an early in-chambers conference can be very useful in ensuring an orderly and a trouble-free trial.

Chapter 21

PRESENTATION AT THE TRIAL

Opening Statements

Each attorney is permitted to give an opening statement to the court, with the petitioner going first. The purpose of the opening statement is to give the court an overview of the issues and the anticipated evidence in support of the party's position on those issues. The respondent gives his opening statement second, but has the right to present his opening statement on his case in chief.

Petitioner's Case in Chief

After the conclusion of opening statements, the petitioner starts the presentation of his or her evidence. The presentation of evidence may be done in a number of ways, but generally it is done by testimony of witnesses. The petitioner's attorney asks the witness, who is usually friendly to his or her client, various questions (direct examination). When the petitioner's attorney is done asking the witness questions, the respondent's attorney is entitled to ask that same witness questions (cross-examination). When the respondent's attorney concludes, the petitioner's attorney may ask any further questions he or she deems appropriate (redirect examination, and so on) until both sides have concluded their questioning. At that point the witness is excused, the next witness is called, and the process is repeated.

Respondent's Case in Chief

After the petitioner rests his case, the respondent's attorney moves forward with her case. She may have already put on much of her case through the cross-examination of the petitioner's witnesses. However, she may have additional witnesses and testimony. The procedure of putting this evidence before the court is the same as in the petitioner's case in chief. When the respondent's attorney concludes the presentation of the respondent's evidence, the respondent will rest. He will tell the judge that the respondent rests by saying, "I have no further evidence to present." If you are the respondent in a divorce action, you may be called to testify during the petitioner's case in chief, but the rules regarding testifying remain the same. The opposing counsel could call you as his first witness to throw you off, so be prepared for going first.

Rebuttal Testimony

After both sides have rested their respective cases, the petitioner is entitled to put on rebuttal testimony, the purpose of which is to rebut any evidence previously unrebutted in the respondent's case in chief. And, of course, thereafter if need be, the respondent can offer re-rebuttal evidence. If rebuttal and re-rebuttal evidence is presented at all, it is usually very short and limited.

Closing Arguments

After the introduction of evidence has been closed, both parties, through their attorneys, are entitled to make closing statements for the purpose of arguing to the court the evidence introduced and the applicable law as applied to the case.

Procedurally, the court allots a certain amount of time for closing arguments. Assuming the court has allotted twenty minutes, the petitioner, who opens or starts, then divides the time between opening and closing. For example, the petitioner's counsel may announce fifteen minutes to open and five minutes to close. The procedure following is that the petitioner argues for fifteen minutes, the respondent argues for twenty minutes, and the petitioner argues for five minutes. The court customarily keeps strict time for closing arguments.

The Court's Verdict

After closing arguments, the court will make its decision on all issues that have not previously been argued upon by the parties. Sometimes the court will make a ruling immediately after closing arguments, but more than not, particularly if there has been considerable evidence or testimony or a lengthy trial, the court will take the case under advisement, which means the Judge wants time to consider and review the evidence and his or her notes before making a ruling. After the trial, the judge will render a verdict. It is very common for a judge to take weeks, even months in some cases to actually issue a verdict. Rarely is a verdict issued at the moment trial ends. After the attorneys receive the verdict, they will draft a final order based on that verdict.

The time a case is under advisement varies, but experienced judges understand the need for prompt rulings and attempt to get the court's order made within days or a few weeks after the conclusion of the case. Usually a case is not under advisement for more than two weeks without some understandable explanation such as other professional commitments of the court, although upon rare occasion it can be considerably longer.

Once the court is prepared to announce its ruling (rendition), a hearing will be set or your attorney will receive the ruling by mail. If there is a hearing, your attendance may or may not be required depending upon the court's policies and your attorney will advise you if you need to be there.

After the rendition is received, one of the attorneys will prepare an order, containing the provisions of the rendition. Quite often the rendition has also included the name of the attorney the court expects to prepare the order and the date by which it was be prepared and presented to the court (entry date). Between the receipt of rendition and the entry date, attorneys for both parties attempt to resolve the form of the order. If resolution is reached, the form of the order is approved and submitted to the court for signature. If resolution cannot be had, any conflicts will be resolved by the court at entry. Thereafter, the final judgment is revised in accordance with the court's instructions and signed by the court. The final judgment becomes your final decree.

Chapter 22

MARITAL PROPERTY

Each state has its own provision for dividing property at divorce. Many divide only property acquired during the marriage; some states include property that a spouse owned before a marriage or received as a gift during the marriage. If you and your spouse are unable to agree on who gets what, the court will divide the property for you.

When you are going through a divorce, you will need to list marital property and separate property. Some property can have a mixed character. Determining whether property is community property or separate property will be very important to your case. In Texas, marital estates are described as follows:

Section 3.001 of the Texas Family Code states:

A spouse's separate property consists of:

(1)   the property owned or claimed by the spouse before marriage;

(2)   the property acquired by the spouse during marriage by gift, devise, or descent; and

(3)   the recovery for personal injuries sustained by the spouse during marriage, except any recovery for loss of earning capacity during marriage.

Section 3.002 of the Texas Family Code states:

Community property consists of the property, other than separate property, acquired by either spouse during the marriage.

Section 3.003 of the Texas Family Code states:

a.   Property possessed by either spouse during or on dissolution of marriage is presumed to be community property.

b.   The degree of proof necessary to establish that property is separate property is clear and convincing evidence.

Please make a list of all separate and community property on the Inventory and Appraisement sheet provided by our office. Remember, if you are making a claim that property is separate property, the burden is placed firmly on your shoulders to prove the separate nature of the property. Proof may consist of a deed, a bill of sale, a cancelled check, a receipt or other documentary proof or testimony that may aid the court to determining whether property is separate or community. The burden of proof to establish that property is separate property is "clear and convincing evidence." These documents showing that an asset is separate property, such as an account statement for every month since date of marriage, must be produced to the other side before a settlement conference and at least sixty days before trial, sometimes earlier.

Chapter 23

INVENTORY AND
APPRAISEMENT

The inventory and appraisement (I&A) is only an overview of your marital estates. It is not designed to be a division of your property or debts. See I&A form attached as Exhibit 2. You should include property in your possession as well as in your spouse's possession. If you are unsure of what your spouse has, do the best you can. Please remember that an I&A is a sworn account of your marital estate. It will need to be updated periodically so that it is as accurate as possible. The document is a summary of your testimony as to your property and debts and can be used against you if you do not take care to ensure it is as accurate. Also, take care as to whether an item is separate or community property because your inventory and appraisement is a judicial admission. Therefore your characterization of property will be binding at mediation or trial. Items that include both community property and separate property portions should be placed in both sections with the appropriate portion in each. When you prepare your I&A, make a copy of the documents you used, as opposing counsel will require these prior to settlement.

The inventory and appraisement should include your proposed value of the property in your estate. If the parties cannot agree on the value of a particular asset, the court will make a decision on the value based on the evidence presented.

Chapter 24

PROPOSED PROPERTY DIVISION

Dividing Property and Debts

The proposed property division is the heart of your request for division of your estate in a divorce. It is the most important document next to the parenting plan if you have minor children. Ask your attorney to prepare this early on. It will give you peace of mind and hopefully once it is completed you will sleep better. This is because you have a much better idea of how you believe your estate should be divided and how to start planning for life after divorce. We will also be working with you on a proposed property division (PPD). See PPD form attached as Exhibit 2. A PPD is an outline of how you would like to see the community estate divided. Separate property items are not to be included in this document. Essentially, a PPD is a spread sheet of the division of your marital estate. It is a list of your community property, community debts with the approximate values and to whom each item should be awarded. The division should be as fair as possible unless you have requested a disproportionate share of the community estate. In our office we combine the I&A and the PPD into one document to present at the time of settlement or trial. This helps save money on attorney fees and is easier for the mediator or judge. Dividing the property can be tedious. You will need to put the most time into this document. This will be your road map on how to settle your case.

In a divorce, your estate will be divided either by agreement or by the court. The Texas Family Code provides that the court should divide your estate in a manner that is "just and right." In many cases, this means an equal division of the property in the estate, however, an equal division is not required. The court can consider many factors when deciding how to divide the community estate, such as the relative income of the parties, the age and health of the parties, and fault in the breakup of the marriage. Based on the specific circumstances of an individual case, the court may award a larger share of the community estate to one of the spouses because that is what the Judge believes is a "just and right" division of the estate. For example, if one of the parties earns over $1 million per year and the other spouse earns $25,000 per year and has primary custody of the children, the court may award the lower earning spouse more of the community property because it is fair. It is important to discuss the possibility of an unequal division of the estate with your attorney early on to prepare for this possibility.

All community property should be brought to the court's attention in the divorce. Any community property that is not divided in the divorce remains as jointly owned property of the parties and either party may request that it be divided by the court in a later proceeding. If any assets are concealed, the court has the authority to award the asset to the innocent party. There are time limits on bringing a suit to divide property after a divorce, so an attorney should be consulted.

In most cases, one of the largest assets in the estate is the family home, and often this is the only major asset in the estate. Deciding on how to divide this asset can be a difficult and emotional process. It is normal for both spouses to be attached to the home because of the time, money and effort devoted to it. Also, many people find that they cannot afford to stay in the home after the divorce for financial reasons. Your attorney can help you come up with a plan on how you want to divide this asset in your divorce.

Chapter 25

TAX CONSIDERATIONS
AND HIDDEN ASSETS

A divorce has important consequences. Custody can affect your taxes, including your right to claim head of household status, dependent exemptions, and child care credit. Support payments may be taxable or deductible. The property division may also affect your taxes. Your certified public accountant (CPA) can advise you about the tax aspects of divorce. If one spouse is hiding assets, it may be necessary to hire a forensic certified public accountant or a private investigator.

In trying to decide how to divide the community estate, the court, the mediator, or the arbitrator may consider the contributions of each spouse to the property, the contributions of each spouse to child care and home-making, the financial resources, the needs of each spouse, and the income and career potential of each spouse. Your lawyer can help you obtain a fair division of property and help you avoid overlooking valuable assets such as pension rights, stock options, or bonuses. It is fine to prepare your Internal Revenue Service tax return on your own—except for the year of your divorce. You need to have a CPA prepare your tax return the year you are divorced. Please consult a CPA on tax issues regarding your divorce. It is always a good idea for your CPA to review the tax language of your decree of divorce before signing.

Investigations in divorce or family law cases include a vast array of issues that must be resolved. The most important issues are typically financial responsibility and child custody. In many family law cases, a spouse will attempt to hide assets in order to avoid relinquishing those assets in a divorce settlement or in an attempt to pay less in child support. In a divorce case, any incriminating evidence, such as evidence of infidelity, hidden assets, and other incriminating data, is most likely located on a mobile device, such as a smartphone, laptop, or tablet. Through forensic imaging of an electronic device, evidence of an undisclosed bank account, credit card, investment, property, or other assets can often be discovered and used as evidence in divorce cases, and therefore you can have access to more property or assets.

When families break apart, sometimes the issues can quickly spin out of control. Allegations of child abuse, sexual abuse, and other claims of spousal misbehavior can quickly come to the forefront. Regardless of what side of the case you are on, the facts matter. In many of these cases, digital data is the key in bringing the truth to light. Hidden bank accounts, undisclosed relationships, or even plans to abduct a child and relocate to a foreign country can be discovered. Sometimes it helps to hire a private investigator who is experienced and has the right tools and skill to uncover the truth.

Chapter 26

RETIREMENT BENEFITS AND SOCIAL SECURITY

Dividing retirement benefits in a divorce can be a very complex matter. If it is not done correctly, you may end up losing out on some benefits that you are entitled to. If you or your spouse have any IRAs, 401(k)s, pensions, or other retirement assets, you should discuss them with your attorney to make sure that you understand what benefits may be available and how you may be able to maximize these benefits for your future financial well-being. Many of these plans require a qualified domestic relations order, which is a court order directed to a plan administrator, to be divided pursuant to a divorce. Qualified domestic relations orders are complicated legal documents, so you should make sure that it is prepared by a qualified legal professional.

Another issue that may come up after a divorce is the effect on Social Security benefits. If you meet certain criteria, when you reach a certain age, you may be entitled to collect Social Security benefits in your own name or as dependents' benefits based on your former spouse's benefits. Whether you are entitled to benefits based on your former spouse's benefits is a matter between you and the Social Security Administration, and your entitlement does not depend on what you and your spouse agree to in the divorce.

Social Security benefits are governed by federal law and not by the state divorce court. The decisions you make regarding Social Security benefits may affect you financially for the rest of your life. If you are divorced, you may qualify to receive Social Security based on your former spouse's employment record.

The following are some basic rules for qualifying for Social Security benefits based on your former spouse's employment record:

1.   You must be at least sixty-two and have been married ten years or more.

2.   The divorce must have been final at least two years before you file for Social Security benefits.

3.   Your former spouse must have reached the age at which he or she is eligible to receive Social Security.

4.   You must be unmarried.

5.   You must not be entitled to a higher Social Security benefit under your own work record.

     If you meet all the above criteria and you have reached your full retirement age, then you qualify for 50 percent of the amount your former spouse is due at his or her full retirement age. If you elect to receive Social Security at age sixty-two, then you qualify to receive 25 percent of his or her benefit. Any benefit you get will not affect the amount your former spouse may receive. If your former spouse dies, you can access a widow's benefit as early as age sixty, as long as you were married for ten years or longer. It is best to consult an attorney or a certified divorce analyst. They are the professionals in maximizing your Social Security benefits.

Chapter 27

FINANCIAL INFORMATION STATEMENT

A form that you will have to complete, if child support or spousal support are at issue in your case, is called the financial information statement (FIS). See the FIS form attached as Exhibit 1. The FIS is essentially a monthly budget depicting your income and expenses. This form will determine the amount of temporary spousal support or child support you will pay or will receive. The important thing to remember when completing this form is that it is a *monthly* budget. That means expenses that do not occur every month (dental bills, prescriptions, holiday expenses, travel costs, etc.) will need to be calculated and prorated in order to make your budget as accurate as possible. There may also be expenses that occur more than once within a month's time. The best way to complete the form so that it is as accurate as possible is to look at your expenses over the year and divide that amount by twelve months. This will ensure that those once-a-year expenses don't break your budget when they do occur. Also, you must attach your three most recent pay statements and your last two tax returns to the form. That is a court requirement. If you are remarried, talk to your attorney about how to complete the FIS form. Usually we ask our clients to list two-thirds of the household expenses for the wife and children and not to include a new husband's expenses or income.

The purpose of the FIS is to provide the court with a picture of your monthly cash flow, both income and expenses, so the court can make decisions about child support and spousal support. The judge in your case needs to know what funds are available for payment of expenses and what expenses need to be paid. It is very important to be as thorough and as accurate as possible when completing this form so that the court has the ability to address your specific financial needs.

Chapter 28

SPOUSAL SUPPORT

Spousal support is also called alimony or maintenance. You or your spouse may be entitled to spousal support depending on the income of the parties, the value of the community estate, and your financial needs. If you and your spouse are unable to agree on support, a judge will decide who should pay it, how much is to be paid, and how long it will continue.

In a divorce case, the court may order one party to pay temporary spousal support while the divorce case is pending. This is very common. It is not the same thing as alimony or spousal maintenance that is paid after the divorce is finalized. The purpose of temporary spousal support is to protect the assets and the credit of the parties while the case is pending. The purpose is usually to make sure that all of the community expenses and liabilities, such as mortgages, utilities, car payments, and credit card payments will continue to be made while the case is pending. The court has broad authority to order temporary spousal support in most cases.

On the other hand, the court has limited authority to order spousal maintenance, or alimony, to be paid after the divorce is finalized. In order to receive spousal maintenance or alimony, a former spouse must meet the eligibility requirements set out in the Texas Family Code. There are also limitations on the amount of the maintenance payments and how long they can continue. The purpose of ordering maintenance or alimony is usually to provide enough support for a former spouse to continue to meet minimum basic needs until he or she can become financially independent. It is important to note that the court has discretion on whether or not to order maintenance. The court will consider factors such as the ability of the spouses to support themselves after the divorce and whether each will be awarded enough assets in the divorce to be able to meet their minimum needs. Alimony is very hard to obtain in court, but if the parties agree on alimony, the court will sign their agreement. Only 15 percent of divorced women nationwide are awarded alimony. In Texas it is a much lower percentage.

The following is a summary of Section 8.051 of the Texas Family Code regarding the Eligibility for Maintenance:

In a suit for dissolution of a marriage, the court may order maintenance for either spouse only if the spouse seeking maintenance will lack sufficient property, including the spouse's separate property, on dissolution of the marriage to provide for minimum reasonable needs and:

1.   The spouse from whom maintenance is requested was convicted of or received deferred adjudication for a criminal offense that also constitutes an act of family violence, as defined by Section 71.004, committed during the marriage against the other spouse or the other spouse's child and the offense occurred:

    A.   within two years before the date on which a suit for dissolution of the marriage is filed; or

    B.   while the suit is pending; or

2.   The spouse seeking maintenance

      A.   is unable to earn sufficient income to provide for minimum reasonable needs because of an incapacitating physical or mental disability;

      B.   has been married to the other spouse for ten years or longer and lacks the ability to earn sufficient income to provide for minimum reasonable needs; or

      C.   is the custodian of a child of the marriage, of any age, who requires substantial care and personal supervision because of a physical or mental disability that prevents the spouse from earning sufficient income to provide for minimum reasonable needs.

Chapter 29

CUSTODY

In Texas, both parties are appointed joint managing conservators unless it is not in the best interest of the child or children. The parent who is appointed the primary joint managing conservator and whom the children will live with is the parent who has the responsibility for making day-to-day decisions. The other parent is also called a joint managing conservator and he or she will have visitation rights and will pay child support. The decisions for the children's education, religion, and nonemergency medical care can be shared by the parents.

Joint Custody

There is no one standard joint custody arrangement. Some parents alternate weeks with the children and others alternate months. Still others divide the children's time unequally, but in a manner that meets the needs of each particular family. Some courts will not allow week-on week-off possession. Every court is different and your attorney will know the rules. Parents who work out these arrangements themselves are usually more creative than courts are when custody is in dispute. Parents often want to know if their children will be called as witnesses. Professionals advise against involving children in court proceedings because it is a very traumatic experience for them. This is equally true whether the dispute is over custody or something else.

Many people incorrectly assume that at a certain age, children have an absolute right to pick the parent with whom they will live. Many courts have developed the custom of interviewing the children. However, the interview alone will not determine the court's decision.

You may want your lawyer to talk to your children. Although opinions vary, many lawyers will refuse, believing that such direct involvement in the case is very hard for children and not in their best interest.

The rights and duties of most parents under the Texas Family Code are summarized below.

At all times each parent has the following rights:

1.   The right to receive information from the other parent concerning the health, education, and welfare of the child

2.   The right to confer with the other parent to the extent possible before making a decision concerning the health, education, and welfare of the child

3.   The right of access to medical, dental, psychological, and educational records of the child

4.   The right to consult with a physician, dentist, or psychologist of the child

5.   The right to consult with school officials concerning the child's welfare and educational status, including school activities

6.   The right to attend school activities

7.   The right to be designated on the child's records as a person to be notified in case of an emergency

8.   The right to consent to medical, dental, and surgical treatment during an emergency involving an immediate danger to the health and safety of the child

9.   The right to manage the estate of the child to the extent the estate has been created by the parent or the parent's family

10.   The duty to inform the other parent in a timely manner of significant information concerning the health, education, and welfare of the child

11.   The duty to inform the other parent if living with a registered sex offender

During their respective periods of possession, the *father* and *mother*, as conservators, each have the following rights and duties:

1.   The duty of care, control, protection, and reasonable discipline of the child

2.   The duty to support the child, including providing the child with clothing, food, shelter, and medical and dental care not involving an invasive procedure

3.   The right to consent for the child to receive medical and dental care not involving an invasive procedure

4.   The right to direct the moral and religious training of the child

The following rights can be allocated exclusively to one parent, independently to both parents, or jointly between the parents:

1.   The right to designate the primary residence of the child

2.   The right to consent to medical, dental, and surgical treatment involving invasive procedures

3.   The right to consent to psychiatric and psychological treatment

4.   The right to receive and give receipt for periodic payments for the support of the child and to hold or disburse these funds for the benefit of the child

5.   The right to represent the child in legal action and to make other decisions of substantial legal significance concerning the child

6.   The right to consent to marriage and to enlistment in the armed forces of the United States

7.   The right to make decisions concerning the child's education

8.   The right to the services and earnings of the child

9.   Except when a guardian of the child's estate or a guardian or attorney ad litem has been appointed for the child, the right to act as an agent of the child in relation to the child's estate if the child's action is required by a state, the United States, or a foreign government.

Having an exclusive right or duty means that a parent can make the decision independently, and the other parent does not have the right to make that decision for the child. When the rights are awarded to both parents, either parent can make the decision. When the rights are allocated jointly between the parents, both parents have to agree on the decision that was made.

When a case referred to as being a contested custody case, this basically means the parents are disputing which parent will have the right to designate the child's residence and which parent will have a visitation schedule and pay child support. In some cases, the issue can be whether or not one parent's visitation will have to be supervised, or in extreme cases, whether there will be visitation at all. Nothing in life is more precious than one's own child. Nothing else can match the depth of the joy, satisfaction, love, excitement, and pride. It is not surprising to learn that well over half of all trials in the family courts are child custody suits.

Best Interest of the Child

If you cannot reach an agreement on child custody issues, the court will make a decision based on the best interest of the child. Below are some elements and guidelines that are taken into consideration when making this determination:

•   Which parent has been the child's primary caretaker. Generally, the court will consider which parent assumed the role of the child's primary caretaker before the divorce when deciding who should be the primary caretaker after the divorce. Often, both parents have shared this responsibility, and in those cases this factor has less weight.

- The quality of the child-parent relationship. If a child has developed a closer bond with one parent, a judge may consider the desires of the child and may be reluctant to award primary custody to the other parent. A consideration in a case like this would be to avoid emotional trauma for the child.

- The presence of abusive behavior. A history of mental and/ or physical abuse against the child, and also against anyone else in the family, will be a big factor that a judge will consider. Judges generally do not want to place a child in a dangerous environment.

- The physical and mental health of the parents and the child. If one of the parties has special needs or an impairment, the judge will likely consider which parent has the ability to provide the appropriate level of care for the child, the ability to meet the emotional and physical needs of the child, and whether living with one parent or the other has the potential to harm the child's development.

- Substance abuse issues. If a parent has an issue with drugs or alcohol, this may create a dangerous situation for the child and a judge will generally take appropriate measures to ensure the child's safety.

- The parenting abilities of each parent. The judge may consider the parenting skills of a parent as well as his or her plans for the child and ability to provide a stable home.

- Ability to co-parent. The efforts of each parent to either encourage the child's relationship with the other parent, or to frustrate that relationship, will be considered by the judge when making a decision on child custody. If one parent is trying to interfere with the other parent's ability to spend time with the child or to communicate with the child, a judge may consider giving primary custody to the other parent. This can be a complicated issue when there is abuse occurring. A parent who is trying to protect his or her child may be viewed as trying to thwart the other parent's relationship with the child. You should discuss these issues with your attorney as soon as possible.

Try to Maintain Continuity between the Parents' Homes

Your child's relationship with both parents is important. It is always beneficial to have the issues involving children resolved quickly so that they can adjust to their new lives and resume a sense of normalcy. After a divorce, there should be a sense of continuity between both homes. Parents should try to maintain the same rules, bed times, meal schedules, and methods of discipline. Maintaining a sense of normalcy and continuity can help children adjust to their new lives and better cope with the divorce.

Restricting Visitation

In appropriate situations, a judge can limit visitation or order that a parent's visitation has to be supervised. Supervised visitation allows a child contact with a parent in a safe environment if it is necessary to ensure the safety and welfare of the child.

You can have a family member supervise visitation if the court will approve, or it may have to be a paid neutral third party, such as those discussed below.

Supervised Visitation Programs

Program	Registration Per Party	Minimum Cost Visit	Cost/Hour Two-hour min. for all	Travel Report	Guest Fee
WATCH 281-635-3664	$50.00	$110.00	$30.00	$50.00	$10.00 per hour
SAFE 713-755-5625	$75.00	$85.00	$60.00 first hour	None	Not allowed
Guardians of Hope 713-542-1110	$75.00	$110.00	$35.00	$40.00	$5.00 per hour
Angel House 713-392-5525	$100.00	Varies	Varies	Varies	$25.00

WATCH Information

There are supervisors available to conduct off-site visitations for days and evenings on both weekdays and weekends.

The owner of the company is a member of Supervised Visitation Network, previously worked for SAFE, and is a family law paralegal. There are four total supervisors on staff.

In cases where there are sexual abuse allegations, the owner would require that there be two supervisors for each visitation. The owner would supervise these visitations with the aid of another staff member who was previously a guard at the prison in Liberty County. No extra charge would be incurred by having a second supervisor.

SAFE Information

They are available for off-site visitations during all reasonable hours on the weekends and beginning at 4:00 p.m. on weekdays.

Their only specific requirement for supervisors is that they must have some form of professional experience with children. Prior to becoming a supervisor they are also required to volunteer and observe for a minimum of two on-site group visits (eight hours total) and a minimum of three private off-site visits. More could be required, based on the individual supervisor's background. In addition to occasional meetings, they also require all supervisors to attend training once per year. The custodial parent is to pick up and drop off the children at the appropriate times.

Any costs incurred during the visitation are to be paid by the non-custodial parent. For example, if the parties want to have visitation take place at the zoo, the supervisor will not be expected to pay the admittance fee.

http://www.victimassistancecentre.com/safesupervised.html

Guardian of Hope Information

They require no specific qualifications or training for the supervisors. The owner of the company is a member of Supervised Visitation Network.

Angel House Information

They are willing to work around nearly any schedule needs that may arise for off-site visitations, both on weekdays and weekends. However, they do not conduct supervised visitation prior to 2:00 p.m. on Sundays.

They require no specific qualifications or training for the supervisors. There are approximately four to five supervisors on staff, and three do off-site private visits. Typically, they require group visits before allowing off-site private visits. However, in cases where the noncustodial parent has sexual abuse allegations they usually require four on-site private visits. These requirements are waived if agreed to by the parties and/or the court.

Chapter 30

KEYS TO BEING
AWARDED CUSTODY

This section is designed to help you understand what criteria are important to a jury or judge when deciding the issue of custody. Yes, a jury of twelve people could decide which parent will have custody. In Texas, having custody is called being the primary joint managing conservator or sole managing conservator. This chapter will help you prepare for mediation, trial, or arbitration. With more fathers obtaining custody of their children, and the law presuming fathers and mothers should be appointed joint managing conservators, the family courts are faced with an increase in custody litigation. Before you file for custody, make sure this is really in your children's best interest. Many times a parent will file for custody just to hurt the other parent, or to obtain leverage in the property settlement. That brings us to a case from a few years ago, where the father pushed hard for custody, saying the child meant everything to him and that the mother didn't care about the little one. He paid over $80,000 in attorney's legal fees pursuing custody. When the mediator mentioned the mother had filed a lawsuit against him for an increase in child support, he said, "All this over one damn kid."

Most primary joint managing conservators seem to be pretty good about tolerating the other parent's visits. Quite a few of the more enlightened parents see the positive benefits of it and are very supportive. Some parents who have primary custody will seemingly do anything in their power to prevent visitation from occurring, but it always hurts the children. Children sense your anxiety. Even nonverbal children pick up the energy between their parents. Seek court intervention if this is happening in your family. If you are the parent thwarting visitation, it could cause you to lose custody. Dads can get custody too, of course, and more and more often they do. According to the Bureau of Labor Statistics 2007 report on the current status of single-parent households, 77 percent are headed by moms and 23 percent by dads. But regardless of whoever takes primary physical custody, they should try to remain supportive of the visitation periods.

The key to a successful visitation is to allow the noncustodial parent and child a sufficient amount of quality time together so that they are able to interact in a naturally close and intimate personal setting. Only in this way can the child develop fully and be grounded.

Clients often ask, "I once had a brief affair. My husband says he will take the kids away from me. Can he?" Misconduct or fault that does not involve the children is seldom significant in determining child custody, but it could be significant, depending on your conduct. Tell your lawyer about these concerns.

The Texas Family Code provides some guidance on which factors should be considered when making a decision in a custody dispute. These sections of the code are listed and sumarized below.

Section 153.131 of the Texas Family Code: Presumption that a Parent will be Appointed Managing Conservator

(a)   (Except in cases of Family Violence) Unless the court finds that appointment of the parent or parents would not be in the best interest of the child because the appointment would significantly impair the child's physical health or emotional development, a parent shall be appointed sole managing conservator or both parents shall be appointed as joint managing conservators.

(b)   It is a rebuttable presumption that the appointment of the parents of a child as joint managing conservators is in the best interest of a child. A finding of a history of family violence involving the parents of a child removes the presumption under this subsection.

Section 153.134(a) of the Texas Family Code: Court-Ordered Joint Conservatorship

If a written agreement of the parents is not filed with the court, the court may render an order appointing the parents joint managing conservators only if the appointment is in the best interest of the child. The following factors are considered:

1.   Whether the physical, psychological, or emotional needs and development of the child will benefit from the appointment of joint managing conservators.

2.   The ability of the parents to give first priority to the welfare of the child and reach shared decisions in the child's best interest.

3.   Whether each parent can encourage and accept a positive relationship between the child and the other parent.

4.	Whether both parents participated in child rearing before the filing of the suit.

5.	The geographical proximity of the parents' residences.

6.	If the child is twelve years of age or older, the child's preference, if any, regarding the appointment of joint managing conservators.

7.	Any other relevant factors.

We always ask the jury to forget what the parents want and look at this matter through the eyes of the child, bearing in mind that we assume that jurors are pillars of this community and want what is best for the child.

If mediation was not succesful, you need to step back to see if there is any way to settle your case short of trial. If you have tried everything but still cannot settle your case, then consider arbitration instead of trial. To speak plainly, I would rather you have a root canal with no anesthesia than go to trial. Sometimes there is no way to avoid it, but please make sure you have explored every option first. Attorneys try to give the appearance of neutrality. However, we are indeed very biased in favor of our clients, as we should be. It's important to begin working together as early in the divorce process as possible at gathering evidence and putting it in presentable form in order to convince the judge or jury that you are the better parent.

One of the issues the court looks at in deciding custody is which parent is more likely to foster the relationship with the other parent. Can you list five things you recently did to foster the relationship with your spouse or former spouse? Two ideas are listed below.

1.	Be sure to give the other parent a card or gift for his or her birthday, Christmas, and Father's or Mother's Day.

2.	If your children are little, have them make the birthday card with glitter and stickers. Have them draw a self-portrait or trace their hand on construction paper. Look online or follow Pinterest for gift projects that are low cost or free. The kids will love making them and have fun at the same time.

You may keep a list of daily events. Custody trials can take from four months to two years to finalize, so keeping a written record of daily events, notes, and questions for your attorney is imperative. This diary should be titled and referred to as an "attorney update" so that the opposing attorney cannot require you to produce a copy to them through discovery. An example of a list of daily events is included as Exhibit 8. Make a list of how you deal with each of the following subjects (compare and contrast):

1.	Quality time with the child. The parent that spends more quality time with the child will have an advantage with the judge or the jury. Giving the child undivided attention and doing wholesome things together is essential. Be honest with yourself. Who does give the child more quality time? Keep a list of indoor and outdoor activities you do with the child. Keep a list of the time the child spends with a nanny, day care workers, or relatives.

2.	Discipline or lack of discipline. We want to show the judge that your method of discipline is more effective. It may only take a firm voice, taking away privileges, or enforcing a time-out to be effective in disciplining your child. Screaming or yelling at a child is not an effective form of discipline. Severely criticizing a child, and thereby damaging a child's self-esteem, is not proper discipline. Some parents administer no discipline whatsoever, letting the child do whatever he wants. Other parents threaten discipline but never follow through. Give us as much detail on the other parent's form of discipline as you can.

3. Education. Stress the importance of education on a daily basis. Assist your children with their homework. Periodically meet with their teacher and after-school teacher to make sure they are doing well. Become a room parent and eat lunch with your child periodically. Give the school a dozen or more self-addressed stamped envelopes for progress and/or homework mailings. This way you will be able to attend parent events at the school, such as Christmas Programs and other special events. Do not depend on the other parent to keep you informed of school activities. It is as much your responsibility to keep up with the child's schedules as the other parent.

4. Encouragement. Praising your children to make them feel wanted. Encourage your children to try to reach their maximum potential.

5. Physical love and affection. Obviously, appropriate love and physical affection for the child, such as hugs, will make a child feel wanted and needed. What are acceptable guidelines for you and your spouse? Bathing or sleeping with a child over two years old is not healthy and will *not* be acceptable to a jury.

6. Attitude. A parent's general attitude is important to the jury. If one parent is consistently negative and criticizes the child

and others, the jury would probably not want the child to remain in such an environment. A very positive, enthusiastic attitude is critical and extremely impressive to a jury. Ask yourself, which parent exhibits the more positive attitude? A jury will scrutinize you and, based on the evidence, will decide whether your attitude is cocky and arrogant or humble. If you appear arrogant or display a self-righteous attitude, your chances of obtaining custody will decrease significantly. Humility is critical for winning custody.

7.   Bad-mouthing the other parent. Because the child will always be one-half of the other parent, it damages a child when one parent criticizes the other in front of the child. Ask yourself, have I criticized the other parent in front of my child? How much has this affected the child? Do not discuss anything negative about the other parent with anyone, including your attorney, if your child or children are present or within earshot.

8.   New romantic interests. Don't have your child around your new romantic interest while you are still married to the child's other parent. There are several reasons for this apart from the obvious moral implications. It may complicate your divorce. It may make the other spouse angry. But the most important reason is that it may hurt and confuse your child. Even if you think that your child and your new friend will get along well, or even if they already do, it is better to not force this new relationship on your child until the divorce is final. Once the divorce is final, you should still take time and go slowly in involving your child in your dating life.

9.   Finances and sacrificing oneself for the child. Frequently, one parent spends money on himself or herself (car, clothes,

computer, vacation, etc.) rather than on the child. It seems there is never enough money to provide everything one needs or wishes. Obviously, financial priorities are critical. Ask yourself, which parent can demonstrate that when the family financial situation would not allow spending money on oneself, that parent made responsible financial decisions so the children would have their needs met?

10. Child's activities. It is important to demonstrate that your child is involved in several healthy activities. Involve your child in scouting, baseball, swimming, soccer, or dance classes and participate from time to time as a coach or sponsor. If the child is extremely young, encourage friends, relatives, or other children in the neighborhood as guests at your home. Be sure you have arranged pickup and delivery to the child's activities and that you attend at least some of the practices, and/or games.

11. Religion. It is important that your child receive proper moral and religious training. Organized religion is critical to the judge or jury. You must set a good example. Various church and synagogue activities are significant in the life of a child. Ask yourself, who is doing a better job of taking care of the moral and religious training of the child? Are you a Sunday school teacher? Are prayers said at meals and at bedtime? If you do not attend a church or synagogue, ask a relative to take them.

12. Instilling the child with proper attitude toward others and respect for law enforcement. Certainly all children need to have great respect for law enforcement, to obey the law, and to be good citizens who contribute to society in a positive

manner. In this vein, children need to learn, for example, not to take toys belonging to other children. Moreover, the attitude of a child is critical, as it is dangerous to raise a child who believes that he or she can be a "taker" in life and never a "giver." Teaching your child not to criticize others and to be tolerant of other children, polite, and well-mannered is very important. Ask yourself, who is doing a better job at teaching the child to respect law enforcement? Who is doing a better job at teaching the child to respect others and to be tolerant of others, and to have a positive attitude, not criticize others and to have good manners?

13. Clean house and yard. It goes without saying that the child needs to live in a clean and organized home—both inside and out. Who does a better job at housekeeping? Does the child have chores?

14. Proper nutrition. Eating healthily is extremely important to a child, especially having fresh fruits and vegetables rather than snack foods. Ask yourself, who does a better job at being sure that the child eats right? Who puts more thought into meals and nutrition? Who prepares the meals? Which parent serves the kids more fast food?

15. Medical and dental care. Proper health care, especially consistent visits to the doctor and the dentist, are very important to all children. If in doubt as to whether a child should see a doctor, it certainly looks better to a jury if you take the child to the doctor. Ask yourself, who takes the child to the doctor? Have either you or the other parent refused medical or dental treatment for the child when such care should have been obtained?

16.   Cleanliness of the children. Keeping the children in clean
        clothes and clean sheets, and maintaining proper hygiene
        are all critical. Ask yourself, who washes the child's clothes?
        Does the child have appropriate clothing? If not, whose fault
        is it? Who bathes the child? Who washes the child's hair the
        majority of the time?

17.   Avoiding favoritism. Nothing can be worse for a child than
        to feel rejection. One surefire way to feel rejected is if the
        child believes that you favor another child. This is extremely
        important, as acceptance and wanting to feel loved and
        needed is nothing less than crucial. Ask yourself, do either
        one of you play favorites? If so, how can it be proven?

18.   Being an excellent listener. Making sure that the voice of
        your child is always heard, and responded to, is also very
        important to a child. Be sure that you do not tune the child
        out so that you can watch your favorite television show.
        Rather, turn the television off and listen intently. There
        is no substitute for showing that you care for what the
        child has to say and how he or she feels, giving a tender
        and loving response. Who is the better listener to the
        child, especially on a consistent basis? How do each of you
        respond to what the child says—by raising your voice or by
        reacting in an understanding manner?

19.   Moral conduct. Juries care very much about the conduct of
        each party regarding moral and immoral acts. Having an
        affair damages you in the eyes of a jury. It also shows that
        your priority in life is yourself rather than your child. How
        do you and your spouse fare with regard to moral conduct
        during the marriage, including separation? Setting an
        example of proper moral conduct for your child is one of

the most important elements for consideration by a judge or jury in awarding custody and visitation.

20.   Stability. When one parent frequently changes jobs, is a drug user or addict or an alcoholic, has a serious mental problem, or engages in criminal conduct, such actions are extremely detrimental to that spouse when they seek custody. Sometimes proving this may be hard, so please make a list of things that might qualify as evidence as you think of them.

21.   Housing. Frequently in child custody jury trials, photographs and videotapes will be shown depicting the housing arrangements of both parents after they are separated. The court will look at the quality, size, cleanliness, play areas, and type of neighborhood. A video of a day in the life of your child is very effective to obtaining custody. This is a very valuable tool.

22.   Patience. Displaying patience on a daily and consistent basis is good parenting. On the other hand, yelling at the child or displaying general impatience will hurt you in front of the jury. Who has displayed the virtue of patience, especially around the child?

23.   Extended family. Having your brothers, sisters, parents, grandparents, as well as nieces and nephews nearby is very important. Who has more relatives in their locality? Does the child get to visit both sides of their family often?

24.   Special emotional needs of the child. Perhaps your child has special emotional difficulties that require particular attention. Ask yourself, who is doing a better job at meeting these emotional needs?

25. Counseling. Everyone has room for emotional improvement. We encourage you to visit with a trained counselor who can help you through this legal process. You will find there are things you can do to help not only yourself, but your children also.

Making a list of things you can do to improve your parenting skills will help you become a better parent. Go over your list with a person you trust, a counselor, friend, or someone from your place of religious worship.

Chapter 31

AMICUS ATTORNEY

The court will more than likely appoint a neutral person, an attorney, to represent the best interest of the child if custody is at issue or there is chronic high conflict. Such a person is called an amicus attorney. Such an advocate is appointed only to represent the best interest of the child. The amicus attorney will likely make a recommendation as to who should be awarded custody, so it is very important to have good communication with him or her. If an amicus attorney is appointed, the fees will be paid by the parties. Each spouse should be prepared to pay one-half of that fee. The final recommendation of the amicus attorney—this neutral voice—could very well affect the outcome of your suit. All written communication between you and the amicus attorney must be reviewed by a member of your attorney's firm before being sent either to you or the amicus attorney. You may communicate directly with the amicus attorney but *never* with the opposing attorney or his or her staff. Most amicus attorneys request a retainer of $1,000 to $2,500 per party at the beginning of their representation, however this is just an initial retainer and the final amount of the fees are often much higher. Usually the parties will split the amicus fee equally, but the court can alter this under certain circumstances. It is important to note that the court can re-allocate the payment of the amicus attorney's fees after a final trial in your case. This can happen if the court determines that it is more appropriate for one party to assume a larger portion of the cost of the amicus attorney because of their behavior during the case or the financial circumstances of the parents.

It is important to know that, while the amicus attorney should ensure that the child's wishes are made known to the court, he or she is not required to advocate for the wishes of the child. The amicus attorney does not have an attorney-client relationship with the child. He or she provides legal services to the court, not the child. It's important to remember that the amicus attorney is appointed to represent the best interests of the child, which may not be the same as what the child desires.

Chapter 32

PSYCHOLOGICAL EXAMINATION OR MENTAL HEALTH EVALUATION

The court could order the parties to submit to a psychological examination. Usually the judge appoints a mental health expert to conduct the examination and the parties are equally responsible for the cost of the evaluation. This cost can average between $3,000 and $5,000 for each party. The psychologist will evaluate the parties and the children and make a recommendation to the court as to which parent should have custody of the children. The psychologist can also make a recommendation to the parties and the court on issues regarding visitation, such as appropriate restrictions and conditions on a parent's right to visitation and when a parent should start having possession of a child overnight.

The psychologist is an important witness. Usually he or she has a PhD (but will at least have a master's degree) and is experienced in counseling parents and children. The psychologist may administer tests and interviews to determine the level of parenting skills, maturity, patience, and attitude of each parent. He or she will also examine the bond between the parent and child and will prepare a written report to assist the judge.

The psychologist will not be biased in favor of one parent and will base his or her opinion on tests and other documentation that solidify the choice of which parent should have custody. Indeed, a good psychologist gives an air of dignity and credibility to your case that no one else can. Good psychologists will also be able to truthfully state that they do not get involved in a child custody case unless they are convinced regarding which party is the better parent—in other words that they are not simply "for hire."

Chapter 33

SUBSTANCE ABUSE EVALUATION

One issue that comes up often in custody cases is substance abuse. Substance abuse issues can range from claims that a parent drinks too much to claims that a parent has a serious problem with illegal drugs such as cocaine, heroin, or methamphetamines. Many parents with substance abuse issues try to hide these problems and deny that they exist. Denying the existence of the problem can lead to severe negative consequences in a custody case, especially when the other parent has irrefutable evidence of the problem. If you have abused alcohol or drugs, a professional should testify that you have this problem under control and that it will not affect your child. A mental health professional who has experience evaluating and treating substance abuse issues can add credibility to a parent's claim that he or she is working to overcome substance abuse issues and that success is likely. You need to confide this matter to your attorney early on so he or she can take remedial steps to correct and to minimize the negative impact on your custody case.

One useful tool in cases involving substance abuse issues is an alcohol and drug evaluation. The goal of this evaluation is to determine whether or not a person has a dependency or an abuse issue with alcohol or drugs.

An alcohol and drug evaluation usually includes the following important goals:

1.   To aid in the formal diagnosis of an alcohol or drug problem

2.   To establish the severity of the alcohol or drug problem

3.   To guide treatment planning

4.   To define a baseline of the patient's status, to which his or her future conditions can be compared

A variety of methods and assessments can be used to determine a client's dependency on or abuse of alcohol or drugs, including medical examinations, clinical interviews, and formal instruments (questionnaires or tests). Each has specific strengths, and the approaches complement each other as they address the four goals stated above.

At alcoholevaluation.net, there is a questionnaire developed to screen individuals for substance dependence and substance abuse. It is used by many organizations, including addiction treatments centers, criminal justice programs, hospitals, other health organizations, and employee assistance programs. It has been determined, after years of use, that this evaluation tool has a 93 percent accuracy rate in identifying individuals with substance dependency disorders.

Many people ask us, "Are my records from counseling or drug rehab admissible?" Unfortunately, the answer is yes, and almost always in custody cases. The cost of the evaluation in 2015 is usually between $500 to $800.

Chapter 34

SOCIAL STUDY

Prior to a custody case being heard before the court, the parties may have to submit to a social study. In Harris County the study is conducted by a social worker employed by the Harris County Domestic Relations office, described in more detail in chapter 37. The social worker meets both parties and the child(ren) by visiting with them at their home. They will contact witnesses (e.g., counselors, teachers, etc.) and will make a written recommendation to the court. Usually the court orders the parties to split the cost of the social study, which will be between $200 and $750 per party in Harris County, Texas in 2015. In counties that do not have a Domestic Relation Office, a private social worker can be agreed upon or appointed by the court. Outside Harris County it's necessary to hire a private social worker, which may cost from $750 to $2500. Certain social workers only work in specific areas and will not travel outside of their preferred radius. Parties can pay to hire their own social study evaluator instead of an appointed social worker. A social study is mandatory in all adoptions and discretionary in custody and visitation disputes.

A social study can be a valuable tool in a contested custody case. The social workers completing the evaluation receive training in how to make their assessment and will write an informed, impartial report with recommendations to the court on what the result of a contested custody case should be. The social worker will usually interview everyone living in both households and will conduct background checks on the parents. The social study report usually provides a detailed analysis of the circumstances of the parties and potential issues that may affect the child.

It is important to remember that the social study evaluation is based on information provided by the parents and on the public records that are available to the social worker. The social worker will not perform substance abuse evaluations or psychological testing. If there are mental health or substance abuse issues involved in your case, you should consider hiring other professionals to address these issues directly.

The Court appointed social worker will make an appointment to visit you and the children at your home. In adoption cases, they will meet with the terminating and adopting parents. In custody or visitation cases, they will meet with both parents or managing conservators. She will look at all of the rooms, but usually does not go through drawers or cabinets. Make sure your home is clean and not full of clutter. They will talk to each child separately, usually without anyone else present. The social worker will also ask for three references so you should have the name and phone number or email address of your references written or typed before the meeting. Notify all of your references before the social worker calls them and tell them to call the legal assistant at your attorney's office if they have questions. The social worker may ask about the first time you drank or used drugs, your religion, your family history and other background information. The social worker will ask you why you want custody or the termination/adoption. Please list the reasons before the appointment.

Once the social worked has completed their interviews and home visits and reviewed the information available to them, they will prepare a written report setting out the information that they received and their findings and recommendations. This written report will be provided to the attorneys and to the Court.

138

Chapter 35

CHILD SUPPORT

If you are making child support payments, do not withhold or delay them if you are having visitation problems. Paying your child support on the date it is due is imperative and you could go to jail for not doing so. The other parent must pay his or her bills on time and any delay in receiving the child support could cause late fees on rent and credit cards. A judge can put a parent in jail for paying thier child support only a few days late. In one case, a father was ordered to pay child support on the first of each month in the final decree of divorce. He always paid five to ten days late. At the time of the hearing, even though he was caught up on payments, the court sentenced him to ten days in jail for paying late. His situation should make it clear that you must not be late in paying child support. If you pay your child support even five days late, it is a violation of your decree of divorce and there may be consequences. It is also disrespectful to the other parent and your child or children.

The guidelines for the support of a child in this section are specifically designed to apply to situations in which the obligor's monthly net resources are $8550 or less. The example assumes the mother was appointed primary joint managing conservator and the father has visitation.

One child	20 percent of the father's net resources
Two children	25 percent
Three children	30 percent
Four children	35 percent
Five children	40 percent
Six+ children	not less than the amount for five children

If your husband makes $8,550 net per month, he will pay $1,710 for one child and $2,125.50 for two children. If his net income is less than $8,550, then it is a simple calculation. If he nets $2,000 per month, he would pay 20 percent, which is $400 per month. He will be allowed to pay half on the first and half on the fifteenth of each month or in the manner in which he is paid at work. So if he is paid weekly, his child support would be $92.31 per week and is due on the day he is paid. If he is paid every Friday, you would receive one check for $92.31 per week, totaling $400 per month.

In many cases, the court will sign a wage withholding order that can be sent to the employer of the parent who is obligated to pay child support. Pursuant to the wage withholding order, the employer will automatically deduct the amount due for child support from the person's paychecks and send it to the state disbursement unit so that the funds can be distributed to the other parent.

If the parent who is paying child support changes jobs, the other parent can request that a wage withholding order be issued to the new employer to ensure that the payment continue to be withheld even after change in jobs.

If the obligor's net resources exceed $8,550 per month, the court shall presumptively apply the percentage guidelines to the first $8,550 of the obligor's net resources. He or she would pay $1,710 for one child and $2,137.50 for the two children.

Without further reference to the percentage recommended by these guidelines, the court may order additional amounts of child support as appropriate, depending on the income of the parties and the proven needs of the child. However, in no event may the obligor be required to pay more child support than the greater of the presumptive amount or an amount equal to 100 percent of the proven needs of the child.

If the parent paying child support has children from another relationship who are not involved in your case, the Texas Family Code allows that parent to pay a lower percentage of his or her income to account for the fact that he or she has other children to support. The percentage of income that a parent who has children in multiple households should pay is set out in the following chart.

TFC Section 154.129: An Alternative Method of Computing Support for Children in More than One Household

	1	2	3	4	5	6	7
0	20.00	25.00	30.00	35.00	40.00	40.00	40.00
1	17.50	22.60	27.38	32.20	37.33	37.71	38.00
2	16.00	20.63	25.20	30.33	35.43	36.00	36.44
3	14.75	19.00	24.00	29.00	34.00	34.67	35.20
4	13.50	18.33	23.14	28.00	32.89	33.60	34.18
5	13.33	17.86	22.50	27.22	32.00	32.73	33.33
6	13.14	17.50	22.00	26.60	31.27	32.00	32.62
7	13.00	17.22	21.60	26.09	30.67	31.38	32.00

Numbers in the far left column indicate the number of other children the obligor has a duty to support who are not before the court in the current action. Numbers across the top indicate the number of children before the court. If the other parent is obligated to pay child support, it will be reduced from the standard 20 percent (for one child) to 17.5 percent There is a chart promulgated by the attorney general's office on our website that provides further details.

Under the current child support guidelines, the amount of child support for one child will be set at 20 percent of the paying parent's net income. The percentage applied to the parent's income increases if there is more than one child before the court. If that parent has other children who are not before the court, the percentage applied to his or her income decreases. For example, under the current child support guidelines, if a parent has one child before the court and a second child who is not before the court and whom the parent has a duty to support, that parent will pay 17.5 percent of their net income as child support for the child before the court.

Many counties have established courts called IV-D Courts. IV-D Courts are courts where the primary focus is on lawsuits relating to child support involving the office of the attorney general. Each court is identified by number.

Chapter 36

AVOID CONFLICT OVER CHILD SUPPORT ISSUES

What Not to Tell Your Child

Your child should be kept completely away from any child support problems. It can be very damaging for a child to know that the money for his or her support is causing problems, or that a parent is more concerned about the money than about the child. Do not tell your child the following, for example:

> "I may not be able to give you a birthday present if your father does not pay his child support;" or

> "I cannot afford to buy new shoes because your mother is late in paying child support."

Do not use your child as a messenger. Do not ask your child to deliver the child support to the other parent. Support should never be paid to the child.

For the Paying Parent

If you are the paying parent, make the payments on time. Pay only through the Child Support Disbursement Unit at Texas Child Support Disbursement Unit, P.O. Box 659791, San Antonio, Texas 78265-9791, on or before the due date in the order or decree. If you are employed, you may wish to have the support deducted directly from your wages through a wage-withholding order, for both the temporary and the final orders. If you are responsible for maintaining health insurance on the child and for paying part of the uninsured medical expenses, treat those obligations just as seriously as the regular support payments. Failure to comply with these responsibilities can result in your being jailed or fined. Remember that the court looks at your ability to pay not just by your actual job history, but also by what you are capable of earning. If you do not work but are capable of working, the court may require child support based on what you could be earning.

For the receiving parent

If you are the receiving parent, do not ever accept direct payments. Don't forgive unpaid, court-ordered child support (legally, it cannot be done). Realize that the date child support is due to the child support division is not the date you will receive it, unless it was paid early. If you do not receive child support on time, notify your attorney and request prompt action in whatever form he or she deems appropriate. Do not involve your child in your efforts to collect child support. Never request your child to ask his or her father for a child support check.

Chapter 37

HARRIS COUNTY
DOMESTIC RELATIONS OFFICE

The Domestic Relations Office (DRO) is committed to serving families in Houston, Texas and the surrounding region by focusing on the needs of children involved in family litigation. The office provides services when a Harris County Family District Court has jurisdiction. Harris County has one of the best domestic relations offices in Texas. Other counties have tried to model their domestic relations office after Harris County's. David Simpson is currently the executive director and he should be applauded for his contribution to helping so many families. The office is divided into four divisions, each having the specific duties discussed below. You may contact the DRO to assist with any of the following matters.

The legal enforcement division provides services to ensure children receive both emotional and financial support from both parents. Legal services are offered for parents seeking to enforce parenting time with their child or seeking to establish, enforce, or terminate child support. In addition, this division manages the FOCAS program that provides early intervention services for the Texas Integrated Child Support System.

The family court services division prepares social studies, evaluations regarding adoption of a child, conservatorship of a child, visitation and the home of any person seeking conservatorship, possession or adoption of a child. The study is governed by Subchapter D, Chapter 107 of the Texas Family Code and is only prepared in response to a court order. The social study provides the judge with impartial information and a recommendation as to what action should be taken in the child's best interest. A court may order an issue-based investigation (IBI) when seeking immediate answers to specific questions and not a complete social study. The IBI provides specific information (e.g., interview of a child, home visit, criminal records, CPS records, etc.) to the court in less time than required for a complete social study.

The family dispute resolution division provides services to assist families with resolving their disputes outside of the courtroom. Family mediations and access facilitation addressing conservatorship, parental rights, possession, and financial issues are offered by certified mediators. Parent conference services assist parents in high conflict situations.

The community supervision unit provides probation services in the Family District Courts for parents who have been found in contempt for violating a court order pertaining to children. Parents report monthly to an assigned officer and demonstrate compliance with the terms and conditions of their probation.

Chapter 38

MODIFICATION

"**I** want to move out of state and take our child with me. Will I be able to?"

Whether a parent is allowed to move away with a child depends on which court your case has been assigned to and the facts of your case. Most courts do not allow the children to move out of Harris County and contiguous counties if the other parent is involved.

Some things in your final decree of divorce can be modified, changed by the judge after a hearing on child custody. Child support and visitation are a few of the issues that can be modified but only if you can show there has been a change in circumstances. Some orders are not modifiable, such as the division of your property.

Our family system is only set up to react, not to be proactive. The court cannot look at bad things that might happen to the child in the future. That is why it is so hard to change custody. At the time of a divorce or paternity suit, the burden of proof for awarding custody is: who is the better parent? Once custody has been established, it is very difficult to change. It is more involved. To meet the burden of proof on a modification, you must show that the modification is in the best interest of the child as well as one of the following:

1.   The circumstances of the child, a conservator, or other party affected by the Order have materially and substantially changed since the earlier of:

    a.   The date of rendition of the order; or

    b.   The date of the signing of a mediated-to-collaborative law settlement;

    c.   An agreement on which the order is based.

2.   The child is at least twelve years of age and has expressed to the court in chambers, as provided by Section 153.009 of the Texas Family Code, the name of the person the child would prefer to have the exclusive right to designate the primary residence of the child; or

3.   The conservator who has the exclusive right to designate the primary residence of the child has voluntarily relinquished the primary care and possession of the child to another person for at least six months.

A modification requires a much higher burden of proof because it is much harder to change custody. The judge or jury may think you are the better parent by far, but you have not shown that the circumstances of the child, or either parent, have materially and substantially changed since the last order.

As stated above, the Texas Family Code has a specific provision that allows a child who is twelve years of age or older to tell the judge who he or she wants to live with. Many people misunderstand this provision to mean that if the child wants to live with them, they have met their burden of proof in a custody case. However, the judge is not required to follow the child's recommendation as to which parent they want to live with. The judge does not have to rule that the parent the child chooses to live with will be the primary parent if it is not in the child's best interest. This means that even if your child says that she wants you to be the primary parent, you may still need to go through the process of a trial to prove that it is also in the child's best interest.

This can be a very difficult process for a child. In most cases, the child feels placed in the middle and does not want to make this decision. Most professionals would agree that it is better for the parents to resolve their disputes without putting their child in the middle. However, if your child is twelve years of age or older and is adamant about where he or she wants to live, it is important to understand the reason for his or her request. It's also important to realize that there may still be a long battle ahead that will take a huge emotional toll on everyone involved.

The right to designate the primary residence of the child is not the only provision of an order that can be modified. The other provisions, such as those for possession and access and the rights and duties of the parents, are all subject to modification. The same burden of proof applies to these issues. You should discuss your goals in a suit to modify an order with your attorney. A suit to modify an order relating to a child can be a costly and time-consuming endeavor. You need to make sure that your goals are realistic and in the best interest of your children and yourself.

The provisions regarding child support can also be modified. The Texas Family Code has special provisions regarding the modification of child support that make this type of modification substantially easier. This issue must be considered in any suit to modify a previous order. In most cases, when one parent files a suit to change custody, the other parent will almost always file a counterpetition seeking an increase in child support. This is a possibility that should be considered when filing any suit to modify a previous order.

Chapter 39

HANDLING THE DETAILS AFTER DIVORCE

Once the divorce settlement, or in the case of a trial the verdict, is completed, you will need to complete the transfer of property. This will include executing real estate documents, authorizations, transferring personal property, and modifying insurance policies. The following are items that should be done after a divorce:

1. Remove the other spouse's name from any joint bank accounts

2. Cancel any joint credit card accounts

3. Execute and record necessary real estate documents

4. Transfer titles of vehicles, or sign a power of attorney for the transfer

5. Signing promissory notes between spouses to guarantee payment of debts

6.   Issuing Wage Withholding Orders for child support

The following are closing documents that may need to be done:

1.   Power of attorney to transfer motor vehicle

2.   Application for Texas certificate of title

3.   Special warranty deed

4.   Special warranty deed with encumbrance for owelty of
        partition

5.   Deed of trust

6.   Real estate lien note

7.   Deed of trust to secure assumption

8.   Mineral deed

9.   Royalty deed

10.   Real estate title letter

11.   Assignment of escrow funds

12.   Assignment of utility deposits

13.   Assignment of interest

14.   Irrevocable (stock/bond) power

15.   Release of judgment

16.   Operating trust agreement for jointly owned property after divorce

17.   Security agreement with collateral pledge and appointment of escrow agent

18.   Unsecured note

19.   Note (secured by security agreement)

20.   Security agreement

21.   UCC-1 financing statement

22.   Change of beneficiary (life insurance)

23.   Change of certificate of coverage (health insurance)

24.   Release of claim to exemption for child of divorced or separated parents

25.   Change of address

26.   Transfer under the Texas Uniform Transfers to Minors Act

27.   Deed without warranty

28.   Quitclaim deed

Chapter 40

ALTERNATIVES TO DIVORCE

Sometimes divorce seems the only solution, so you file. Sometimes it takes the start of a divorce to motivate people to make an effort to save their marriage. It is fine to try to reconcile after you file. If you have filed for divorce, don't be embarrassed to tell your lawyer you are interested in exploring reconciliation. An experienced attorney knows how important it is to exhaust all possibilities of saving your marriage.

Depending on your circumstances, you may wish to consider alternatives to divorce: marriage counseling, annulment, or separation. For some people, divorce is not an option because of religious, financial or health insurance considerations. Although there is no legal separation in the State of Texas you can live apart from your spouse. You can file an IRS tax return married filing separately or married filing jointly. If you and your spouse separate, it is best to enter into a separation agreement. A separation agreement is a contract between the spouses that can provide for spousal support, child custody-visitation rights, and a division of the property acquired during the marriage. A properly written agreement can be enforced by courts if a party does not comply. If the parties later divorce, it may be included in the divorce judgment.

The following are some issues that can be included in a separation agreement:

1.   Child custody and support

2.   What religion the children observe

3.   Division of property

4.   Whether the parties can date

5.   Inheritance rights

6.   Life insurance

7.   Medical and dental expenses

8.   Payment of debts

9.   Pension rights

10.   Right to live apart

11.   Alimony

12.   Temporary use of property

13.   Temporary spousal support

14.   Who will vacate marital residence

15.   Injunctions (Chapter 3)

It is a good idea to maintain separate bank accounts during a separation. If you have a separation agreement, you should send copies of the agreement to your bank, broker, creditors, and other financial institutions that you and your spouse do business with so they have notice of your agreement. You also need to make sure that you are protecting your credit during a separation. We recommend putting a freeze on all joint credit accounts and sending a letter to all creditors stating that any changes to joint accounts will require signatures from both spouses.

If the parties cannot agree to a separation agreement or if your spouse refuses to move out of the marital residence, or pay spousal support, you will have to file for divorce. Some spouses will choose to live apart while they are trying to reconcile. We can draft a postnuptial agreement that is a contract between you and your spouse setting out the terms of your separation. You could also enter into a partition agreement that divides your assets and liabilities now even though you are not divorcing at this time. You would still be married but financially you are separated.

Chapter 41

RECONCILIATION

E ven after a spouse has filed for divorce, many spouses want to continue to try to make their marriage work. The information provided in the next few chapters may be helpful in saving your marriage if you would like to try. There are a lot of resources available to spouses who are having marital problems. We do not have all of the answers, and the advice and information provided will not work for everyone. We just want to share what we have learned from years of helping people through the painful process of divorce and of sharing ideas and information that have helped repair broken relationships.

Stages of Marriage

There are many stages of marriage, but we have summarized the most significant stages, which will be discussed below: (1) romance, (2) when reality sets in, (3) developing unhealthy habits or learning a healthy way to deal with conflict, and (4) learning to live together. Due to the high divorce rate, many couples do not make it to the fourth stage.

Romance

Most are familiar with the first stage, the romance stage. Life was so wonderful, and we couldn't stand to live without each other. Our thoughts often turned to the other when we were not with them. We had fallen in love and knew that this was the person we wanted to spend the rest of our life with. Little differences between us were cute and endearing.

Reality Sets In

At some point those little differences started to annoy us. We felt bothered by some of those same things that may have been cute a short time earlier. The self-talk in the back of our mind started wondering why our spouse couldn't be more like us. During this stage, we start to realize that our spouse is not the perfect person that we had envisioned him or her to be. Sometimes, especially if our romance stage has been particularly intense, we are hurt deeply by this stage. Several of the key causes of marital conflicts are detailed in an excellent book entitled *Stress and Marriage*, by Dr. Lyle Miller. Perhaps the problem lies with the detonations of the romantic illusions that once enabled the spouses to ignore faults they now find intolerable. Sometimes we marry our own romanticized creations but (surprise) are disappointed when dealing with a real person with real shortcomings.

Unrealistic expectations of our partners are common when the reality sets in, and the marriage will fall apart if you do not learn to operate as a team. We realize that the expectations we had of the perfect marriage were not going to happen. For some, this realization is too heart wrenching, and they give up on the marriage and divorce during this second stage.

Bad Habits

Many people stick with it and try to work through their problems during this stage. They seek the counsel of family, friends, clergy, and marriage family counselors. Some of these people find the key they are looking for from these resources. Many others continue to struggle, and their troubles worsen. Often the marriage deteriorates more deeply due to drug, alcohol, or other addictions. Sometimes a party has an extramarital affair.

This third stage is where many couples find themselves considering separation or divorce. When children are involved, this stage is particularly difficult on them. Regardless of whether the couple stays together or divorces, the children often believe it is their fault despite assurances to the contrary. The effects of divorce on a child cannot be over emphasized. The pain is so intense that it is common to only want it to *stop*. Much like the pain of a toothache that consumes your whole being, you cannot seem to think of anything else besides stopping the pain. One spouse may be pushing hard for the divorce while the other wants to stop the divorce.

If the couple ends the marriage at this point and the spouses remarry other partners, they are more likely to experience the effects of divorce with their second or third spouse.

Learning to Live Together

At this stage, couples either learn how to blend two lives together in a healthy way, or else they accept dysfunctional, unhealthy manners. Most people whose marriages end in divorce are not bad people. Rather, they are often people who never learned the proper tools for a happy marriage. How can you determine if your marriage is worth saving? Talk to your pastor or Elder at your place of worship and ask for help. Can you and your spouse attend a marriage seminar or retreat? We have a partial list in the chapter titled "Alternatives to Divorce." If you find a good marriage seminar, please e-mail our office with the details so we can add it to our list.

Sometimes, as much as you want to save the marriage, you cannot do it if you do not have the cooperation of your spouse. This is when you have to help from a distance. If your spouse has an alcohol or drug problem or refuses treatment for a mental illness, you may have to learn to care from a distance. You cannot fix the problem. Have you ever heard the phrase, "You can lead a horse to water, but you can't make it drink"? I think I can; I can put an IV in the horse to make him drink or stuff a hose in his nose. But the point is that I really can't, and neither can you. You cannot fix the problem when your spouse refuses to participate or co-parent, but you can learn how not to make the problem worse. Many times we exacerbate the problem because we do not know any better. You fall back into the unhealthy "dance" you and your spouse did during marriage. You may swear you are not the problem, but you may be part of the problem or at least contribute to the problem. In every relationship all parties contribute to the breakdown. Everyone is contributing to what is happening. Look at what your part is. If you believe you have tried everything, consider using a parenting facilitator or a parent coordinator. This is discussed in more detail later in the book.

Marriage Workshops

We have listed several options for marriage workshops and weekend seminars below. We specifically have not listed counselors because you should get referrals from the list of approved providers from your health insurance. If you have no health insurance, contact the United Way, your church or place of worship, Houston Area Women's Center, or the Hope and Healing Center.

1. Couples Workshop. Attend a couples workshop or retreat. Some possibilities are: Retrouvaille workshop. Please go to www.retrouvaille.com, or call (800) 470-2230 for more details. Please check with the counselor to see if there are any upcoming weekends you could attend. Retrouvaille clearly works. One third of attending couples in Michigan over the last decade had already filed for divorce, yet 80 percent of nearly 600 couples rebuilt their marriages. Retrouvaille is also a way to foster reconciliation among separated couples. In the Dallas-Fort Worth area, 40 percent of 817 couples were living apart when they went. However, 70 percent of the whole group saved their marriages! Retrouvaille is such a marriage saver that it has saved 80 percent of nearly 50,000 couples who have attended in Canada and the United States. To learn more, call toll-free (800) 470-2230.

2. Family of Origin Workshop. The Family of Origin Workshop's purpose is to provide safe and purposeful exploration of belief systems and provide experiences that help form a bridge to new and healthy functioning. It is not a marriage retreat, but is a workshop to work on the individual. This may be necessary before a marriage workshop can be successful. For most people the blueprint of adult life was largely formulated during childhood. This can shape adult behaviors and belief systems that are unhealthy, making a meaningful relationship next to impossible. Working through these issues can be very helpful. Call Laura Swann at 512-775-4210 or David Clemons at 512-825-3283 for more information or visit www.fooworkshop.com.

3.   Life Marriage Retreats. A four day marriage retreat that provides the perfect convergence of time, results and price. It is designed for couples seeking to take their relationship to the highest possible ground and those who might be experiencing significant relationship distress. Attendance is limited to only a few couples to ensure great group dynamics and maximum personal attention. This retreat offers a balanced amount of training, private sessions, exciting experiential activities and relaxing free time. The retreats are offered at three locations – San Diego, California, Sundance, Utah and Lake LBJ, Texas. For more information call 877-376-7127 or visit www. lifemarriageretreats.com.

4.   The Meadows. A week-long workshop that serves to help couples explore their relational difficulties in a safe environment and learn how to work together to heal their relationships. Participants learn how to enjoy working together with their spouses. To learn more about this workshop please visit www.themeadows.com or call (800) 244-4949.

5.   A seven-session workshop for couples is based on the book, *Hold Me Tight: Seven Conversations for a Lifetime of Love*, by Dr. Sue Johnson. *Hold Me Tight* is based on Emotionally Focused Therapy (EFT), a short-term, structured approach to helping couples strengthen and deepen their emotional bond. In this workshop, couples will practice relationship-building conversations in class, work through take-home exercises, and watch demonstration videos to witness other couples learning to step out of negative cycles and

create a stronger, more loving relationship. For more information, please call Alex Avila at 720-316-7771 in Littleton, Colorado. Or visit www.EFTResourceCenter.com and click on Hold Me Tight Program for more details and registration.

6.   High Conflict Resolution. Attend High Conflict Resolution Classes with Sondra Kaplan, (713) 780-1478, and Judith Miller, (713) 686-9194. They deal with a lot more than just high conflict. Hopefully they will teach you how to communicate better and heal some of the past.

7.   Dr. Ed Silverman, family counseling. Located at 14550 Torrey Chase Blvd., #630, Houston, Texas 77014. For more information call (281) 444-4494.

8.   Dr. Jean Guez, family counseling. Located at 3000 Weslayan St., Houston, Texas 77046. For more information call (713) 552-9500.

9.   The Clearing. A weekend retreat that allows married couples of all ages and all faiths to take a break from the rigors of daily life and clear the barriers to having the marriage they've always wanted. The organization's Marriage Restoration Retreats provide couples with expert intensive counseling in a serene, safe, sequestered environment. For more information visit www.clearingretreat.org or call (979) 885-8121.

10.   Parenting Facilitator or Parenting Coordinator. Contact Rick Goldberg (713) 306-8700, Allyson Bruphacher (281) 398-0505 or Scott Gammeter (281) 440-9661. A parenting coordinator is a professional psychologist or a lawyer

assigned by the court who helps to manage ongoing issues in child custody and visitation cases. Parenting facilitation is a child-centered dispute resolution service that assists parents in developing and implementing workable parenting plans when they are unable to do so on their own.

11.   Marital-Skill Training. How popular is marital-skill training? More than fifty different programs are listed on the website of the Coalition for Marriage, Family, and Couples Education (www.smartmarriages.com). The programs listed are widely available and often cited as standouts by mental health professionals.

12.   PREP (Prevention and Relationship Enhancement Program) is a twelve-hour course offered at locations across the country. Call (800) 366-0166 for local classes or check the website https://www.prepinc.com.

13.   PAIRS (Practical Application of Intimate Relationship Skills). Options run the gamut from a one-day workshop to an intensive 120-hour program. Available in many US cities and abroad. Call 888-724-7748 or check the website: www.pairs.com.

14.   Marriage Encounter. Marriage Encounter is advertised as the most successful marriage saver. It is active in a dozen denominations. In some sixty-one studies, couples have been interviewed before and after the weekend retreat. The surveys found that nearly nine out of ten couples fell back in love with each other. More importantly, they learned communication skills that permanently improved their marriages. To learn more about Marriage Encounter, call (800) 795-LOVE (5683), or visit http://www.wwme.org/

15. National Institute of Relationship Enhancement. Love Skills for Couples workshops are intended for couples who wish to increase overall relationship satisfaction and for couples who want to begin to open channels of caring and love in their relationships. Take a weekend for just the two of you to nurture your relationship. Concentrate on nothing else. Give it all you have. On the first day, you learn to fully express yourself, understand at a deep level, find and express positives, and change conflict patterns. On day two, you build on the core skills, learn effective problem solving, replace nagging with reinforcement, stop patterns of conflict, and build affection activities. The Relationship Enhancement Program has been identified by a Purdue University Study to be one of the most effective marriage enrichment programs for improving relationships. For more information call (301) 680-8977 or visit www.nire.org.

16. Meetings. We suggest a face-to-face meeting without the kids for a minimum of two hours per week to work on your relationship. Ask a professional or someone from your church or place of worship to help facilitate this meeting. Read the book *The Five Love Languages*, by Gary Chapman, and do the assignments at the end of each chapter together.

Chapter 42

STAYING HEALTHY

As we mentioned at the beginning of this book, we are an advocate of the holistic approach to divorce. One of our goals is always to help our clients get through the process in a healthy manner and, hopefully, find a way to become a better person at the end of the process. This chapter has some advice and words of wisdom that come from many years of experience in dealing with conflict.

At some point, it may be necessary to disconnect from your spouse. We hope your case never gets to this point, but if the relationship is toxic, you need to take a time-out. It is a hard habit to break, but it may be necessary. You may have to put call block on your phone or e-mail block on your computer. You may only be able to communicate during the divorce through the Our Family Wizard or Custody Junction Co-Parenting website, until you learn to treat each other with respect. You can visit the organization's websites here: http://www.ourfamilywizard.com/ofw/index.cfm/parents/ and http://www.custodyjunction.com/.

If your spouse's e-mails are causing you extreme stress, set up a new e-mail account that only he or she uses. That way you do not have to respond that minute. You could check the e-mail at set times. If you are having a nice dinner with your daughter when you receive a text or e-mail that is hateful, why allow it to ruin your meal? You and your spouse have argued for so long that it is a habit or a pattern that is familiar. Breaking that habit after so long is very hard. Also, we have all developed a fairly urgent need to respond to e-mails, text messages, and phone calls quickly, especially those from the other parent. This need to respond creates anxiety until we have responded, but unfortunately, there is a never-ending stream of things that require our response.

If we allow these messages to force us to respond almost as soon as they come, then we become driven by the need to respond. Our day becomes responsive or reactive rather than driven by conscious choices. We flit from one task to another, one response to another, living a life driven by the needs of others. You do not need to respond. This is contrary to how you lived as husband and wife, but in moving through the divorce process it may be imperative for you to set new boundaries. You must wean yourself from this need to respond to the other parent immediately. By having a designated e-mail address just for the parent of your child, you can control when you respond. Another aspect of responding immediately is that you may respond to the other parent out of habit or without much thought. This may not be in your child's best interest or yours. Most of the information in the next chapter comes from a book called *The Age of Distraction* by Leo Babauta. We recommend this book. In using the author's recommendations here, we have changed some of the information to apply to the legal process. The author is happy to share with you the digital version of his new book *Focus*. The free version is simple to access: it's twenty-seven chapters that you can download free of charge, without having to give an e-mail address or do anything else. It isn't copyrighted, and you can share it with as many people as you like. Google Leo Babauta to download a copy. The book is about finding the focus you need to work on what's important, to reflect, and to find peace. This is especially hard to do when going through a divorce.

Breaking a Bad Habit

Let's briefly cover some quick strategies you can use to break a bad habit:

1. Figure out what triggers you to repeat this bad habit. List these triggers.

2. Find a new positive habit to replace the old response for each trigger. For example, with quitting smoking, you may need a new habit for stress relief (running), a new thing to do after meetings (write out your notes), a new thing to do with coffee in the morning (reading), and so on.

3. Create positive feedback for the new habit. If the new habit you try to develop is something you don't enjoy, you'll quit trying before long. But if it's something enjoyable, and it gives you positive feedback, you are more likely to stay with it. Praise from others is also a good positive feedback, and you'll want to engineer your habit change so that you get almost instant positive feedback.

4. Create instant negative feedback for the old habit. If you are trying to cut down your computer time, you want to put in place some instant negative feedback if you go online or stay online too long. You could make it a rule that you have to call someone to tell them you have stayed online too long, for example. There are lots of kinds of negative feedback: maybe you'll have to give up your computer time for the next two days or something like that.

5. Repeat the positive-feedback cycle as often as possible for the new habit. After a few weeks, it will become a new habit and the old one will be (mostly) licked.

"Life is a series of natural and spontaneous changes. Don't resist them—that only creates sorrow. Let reality be reality. Let things flow naturally forward in whatever way they like."

—Lao-tzu

Learn to Go with the Flow

No matter how much structure we create in our lives, no matter how many good habits we build, there will always be things that we cannot control—and if we let them, these things can be a huge source of anger, frustration, and stress.

The simple solution: learn to go with the flow.

For example, let's say you've created the perfect peaceful morning routine. You've structured your mornings so that you do things that bring you calm and happiness. And then a water pipe bursts in your bathroom and you spend a stressful morning trying to clean up the mess and get the pipe fixed. You get angry. You are disappointed, because you didn't get to do your morning routine. You are stressed from all these changes to what you're used to. That in turn ruins your day because you are frustrated for the rest of the day.

Not the best way to handle things, is it? And yet if we are honest, most of us have problems like this, with things that disrupt how we like things, with people who change what we are used to, with life when it doesn't go the way we want it to go.

Go with the flow. What is going with the flow? It's rolling with the punches. It's accepting change without getting angry or frustrated. It's taking what life gives you, rather than trying to mold life to be exactly as you want it to be. And what does this have to do with divorce and separation? It's a reality that no matter how much we try to control our environment so that we may focus on what's important, there will be interruptions and distractions. Our environment will constantly change and we cannot completely control it. And so, we must learn to accept this reality, and find focus within a changing environment. Here's how.

1. Realize that you can't control everything. We think we all know this at some level, but the way we think and act and feel many times contradicts this basic truth. We don't control the universe, and yet we seem to wish we could. All the wishful thinking won't make it so. You can't even control everything within your own little sphere of influence—you can influence some things, but many things are simply out of your control. In the example above, you can control your morning routine, but there will be things that happen from time to time (someone's sick, an accident happens, a phone call comes at 5:00 a.m. that disrupts things, etc.) that will make you break your routine. The first step is realizing that these things will happen. Not might happen, but will. There are things that we cannot control that will affect every aspect of our lives, and we must accept that, or we will constantly be frustrated. Meditate on this for a while.

2. Become aware. You can't change things in your head if you're not aware of them. You have to become an observer of your thoughts, a self-examiner. Be aware that you're becoming upset, so that you can do something about it. It helps to keep tally marks in a little notebook for a

week—every time you get upset, put a little mark in the tally. That's all—just keep a tally. And soon, because of that little act, you will become more aware of your anger and frustration.

3. Breathe. When you feel yourself getting angry or frustrated, take a deep breath. Take a few. This is an important step that allows you to calm down and do the rest of the things listed below. Practice this by itself and you'll have come a long way already.

4. Get perspective. If you get angry over something happening—your car breaks down, your children ruin something you're working on—take a deep breath, and take a step back. Let your mind's eye zoom away, until you're far away and above your life. Then whatever happened doesn't seem so important. A week from now, a year from now, this little incident won't matter a single whit. No one will care, not even you. So why get upset about it? Just let it go, and soon it won't be a big deal.

5. Practice. It's important to realize that, just like when you learn any skill, you probably won't be good at this at first. Who is good when they are first learning to write, or read, or drive? No one I know. Skills come with practice. So when you first learn to go with the flow, you will mess up. You will stumble and fall. That's OK—it's part of the process. Just keep practicing, and you'll get the hang of it.

6. Laugh. It helps to see things as funny, rather than frustrating. Car broke down in the middle of traffic and I had no cell phone or spare tire. The best response: laugh at my own incompetence; laugh at the absurdity of the

situation. That requires a certain amount of detachment—you can laugh at the situation if you're above it, but not within it. And that detachment is a good thing. If you can learn to laugh at things, you've come a long way. Try laughing even if you don't think it's funny—it will most likely become funny.

7.   Realize that you can't control others. This is one of the biggest challenges. We get frustrated with other people because they don't act the way we want them to act. Maybe it's our children, maybe it's our spouse or significant other, maybe it's our coworker or boss, or maybe it's our mom or best friend. But we have to realize that they are all acting according to their personality, according to what they feel is right, and they are not going to do what we want all of the time. We have to accept that. Accept that we can't control them, accept them for who they are, accept the things they do. It's not easy, but again, it takes practice.

8.   Accept change and imperfection. When we get things the way we like them, we usually don't want them to change. But they will change. It's a fact of life. We cannot keep things the way we want them to be. Instead, it's better to learn to accept things as they are. Accept that the world is constantly changing, and we are a part of that change. Also, instead of wanting things to be perfect (and what is perfect anyway?), we should accept that they will never be perfect, and we must accept good instead.

9.   Enjoy life as a flow of change, chaos, and beauty. Remember when we asked what perfect is, in the paragraph above? It's actually a very interesting question. Does perfect mean the ideal life and world that we have in our heads? Do we have

an ideal that we try to make the world conform to? If so, it will likely never happen. Instead, try seeing the world as perfect the way it is. It's messy, chaotic, painful, sad, dirty—and completely perfect. The world is beautiful, just as it is. Life is not something static, but a flow of change, never staying the same, always getting messier and more chaotic, always beautiful. There is beauty in everything around us, if we look at it as perfect.

"A good traveler has no fixed plans, and is not intent on arriving."
—Lao-tzu

Be Present with Yourself and Your Family

When you aren't working and you aren't with family, take time to unwind. Take time to allow your brain to slow down. Try meditating. It is quite easy and can be learned from your local Zen Center or from the Internet. So many people watch TV, talk on the phone, or play on the Internet to avoid being alone with themselves. Learn to cherish this time. Try to find ten minutes a day to set aside just for yourself. Take time to reflect and be grateful. Be present with your child. I have heard so many children say, "I do not like going to my dad's; he is always on the computer." Learn to be present.

Imagine you're taking a walk in the park with your child—it's a lovely day, and it's the perfect quiet moment between you and your young one. Then your phone beeps, and you know you have a new e-mail. Well, you've been waiting for something from the boss or client, so you have the urge to check. It's just going to take a few seconds—no problem right?

Well, it's a problem. This small distraction takes you from the moment with your child and back to the world of work. It ruins it, even if only slightly. It also teaches your child that this e-mail is more important than he or she is—you can't make the effort to be totally present with your child because of important work e-mails. That's not the best message to send.

When you're at home, you should not be on the computer while your child is calling for attention. Turn the computer off for stretches of time, and give your undivided attention to your child. When it's time to work, or create, and focus, find a way to do so without the interruptions of children. But the rest of the time, shut off the computer. If you have more than one child, try to find some one-on-one time with each child. Even taking one child for lunch every few months would improve your relationship immensely.

Unsupportive People

Another problem is that people in our lives can sometimes be unsupportive, or flat out against changes we want to make. If one of these people is a spouse or significant other, it can make things very difficult—nearly impossible, sometimes.

This is actually a very common problem. We cannot give you a solution that will work in all cases, but Leo Babauta's book *Focus* lists some things that have worked for him. I share them here in hopes that they might help.

Don't force. When we try to push others to make changes, they often resist. It's not smart to try to force others to adapt to the changes you want to make. Instead, try some of the tips below—setting an example, sharing, asking for help.

Share Why It's Important and How It Affects You

Communications is important here—sit down and talk to the person (or people) about why you want to make these changes, why it's important to you, what it'll help you to do. Share the positive effects as you make the changes, and also share the problems you're facing. This type of open communication can help persuade the other person to get on board with your changes, if done in a nonpushy, nonjudgmental way.

Enlist Their Help

When you ask people to change, they will probably resist, but when you ask them to help *you* change, that's much more likely to succeed. Try as best you can to make it a team effort—working together is a much better proposition than working against each other.

Set an Example

If the other person doesn't want to change, that's OK. Make the changes yourself, and show how great it is. If the other person is inspired by your example, that's even better. Often leading by example is the most persuasive technique there is, but don't be disappointed if the other person doesn't decide to follow your example. Be happy with the changes you've made yourself. If the other person is unsupportive, there might be limits to what you can change. Recognize these boundaries and work within them.

Focus

The book *Focus* is not about divorce but about focus. It is about the distractions of life. The period we are living in is called the age of information, but in another light it can be called the age of distraction. While humanity has never been free from distraction—from swatting those bothersome gnats around the fireplace to dealing with piles of papers and ringing telephones—never have the distractions been as voluminous, overwhelming, intense, and persistent as they are now. Ringing phones are one thing, but e-mail notifications, text messages, Twitter, and Facebook messages, Internet browsing, and mobile devices that are always on and always beeping are quite another. More and more, we are connected, we are up to our necks in the stream of information, we are in the crossfire of the battle for our attention, and we are engaged in a blur of multitasking activity.

With so much competing for our attention, and so little time to focus on real work, it's a wonder we get anything done at all. We've come into this electronic age without being aware that it was happening, or realizing its consequences. Sure, we knew that the Internet was growing and we were excited about that. We knew that mobile devices were becoming more and more present and some people protested being connected and others welcomed being connected. But while the opportunities offered by this online world are a good thing, the constant distractions, the increasingly urgent pull on our attention, the stress of multitasking at an ever-finer granular level, the erosion of our free time and our ability to live with a modicum of peace—perhaps we didn't realize how much this would change our lives.

There's an instant positive feedback to such constant activities as checking e-mail, surfing the web, checking social networks such as blogs, forums, Twitter and Facebook. That's why it's so easy to become addicted to being connected and distracted. You check your e-mail and hey! A new e-mail from a friend! You get a positive feeling, perhaps a validation of your self-worth, when you receive a new e-mail. It feels good to get a message from someone. And thus the instant positive-feedback rewards you for checking e-mail more and more frequently until the addiction is solidly ingrained. During your divorce please do not Twitter or add to Facebook or any social media page. You do not have time to dedicate to this, but more importantly the opposing counsel will use this against you at mediation, temporary orders hearing or trial.

On an ordinary day, we have distractions coming from every direction. But when you are going through a divorce the distractions can be overwhelming. Before your separation there was not enough time in the day, between the children's normal schedule, work, and the demands of raising a family. Once a divorce is filed, there is even less time and there is less help from the other spouse. Add the time necessary to prepare for litigation or mediation and it seems impossible to get it all done. Depending on the complexity of the case, you will need to set aside at least six to eight hours a week to complete the documents necessary to resolve your case.

Constant connectivity and distractions, and a lack of focus, can affect our peace of mind, our stress level our happiness, and makes surviving a divorce much harder. It's important to get away from these constant distractions—we need some quiet, some time to reflect and contemplate, some time for solitude. Without it, our minds are constantly bombarded by information and sensations. That constantly stresses our minds in ways we're not meant to handle.

Rest is important in ways we don't often think about. We need to detox from stress, and we need to recharge our mental batteries. Quiet, solitude, and reflection lead to greater happiness when they are a part of our daily lives. What you do during this time—read, write, run, nap, sit, watch, listen, have a quiet conversation, play, study, build—isn't as important as the simple fact of having that time of disconnection.

Here's a little exercise that might prove useful: as you read this chapter, how many times were you distracted or tempted to switch to another task while reading?

How many times did you think of something you wanted to do, or check your e-mail, or other favorite distractions? How many times did you want to switch, but resisted? How many different things made a noise or visual distraction while you were reading? Did anyone or anything get your attention?

In an ideal world, the answers to all those questions would be zero. You'd be able to read with no distractions and completely focus on your task. Most of us, however, have distractions coming from all sides, and the answers to this little exercise will probably prove illuminating.

So how do we go about disconnecting? There are varying strategies, and no one strategy is better than another. We won't be able to tell you what will work best for you; we suggest you experiment and find a method that fits your needs and situation best. Often that will be a hybrid approach, which is perfectly fine. Every person is different, and no cookie cutter approach will work for us all. When you are working on your divorce, you may want to try some of the ideas set out below.

1. Unplug. Just unplug your network connector or cable, or turn off your wireless router, or go to your connections settings and disable them temporarily. Close your browser and open another program so you can focus on creating without distraction. Do this for as long as you can.

2. Set aside two hours at least three times a week to work on your divorce. Ask your attorney what you should work on so you are not focusing on low priority tasks.

3. Have a disconnect time each day. It's like setting office hours in that—you set the times that work best for you, except you are setting downtime hours. You can even let people know about these times. Let's say you are disconnected from 8:00 to 10:00 a.m. each day, or from 4:00 to 5:00 p.m., or perhaps any time after 2:00 p.m. Tell people your policy, so they'll know you won't be available for e-mail or instant message (IM), and use this time to create.

4. Work somewhere without a connection. For us, this might be the public library—while it has computers with Internet access, there's no wireless in our library. Some coffee shops don't have wireless connection. Some of you might have to look for a good spot that's quiet but doesn't have free

wireless. Go to this disconnected zone to create, or perhaps to just relax and enjoy the quiet.

5.   Get outside. Leave your devices behind and go for a walk, or a run, or a bike ride. Enjoy nature. Watch a sunset; go to the beach, or a lake, or river, or forest. Take your child, or spouse, or friend. Recharge your batteries, reflect, and contemplate.

6.   Leave your mobile device behind or shut it off. When you're on the go, you don't always need to be connected. Sure, the iPhone and Android and Blackberry are cool, but they just feed our addictions, and they make the distraction problems worse than ever. If you're driving, shut off your device. If you're meeting with someone, turn off the device so you can focus on that person completely. If you're out with your family or friends and not working, leave the device at home. You don't need to have this personal time interrupted by work or your impulse to check messages from your spouse.

7.   Use blocking software. If you're doing work on the computer, you can use various types of software to shut yourself off from the Internet, or at least from the most distracting portions of it. For example, you can use software to block your web e-mail, Twitter, favorite news sites, favorite blogs, and so on—whatever your worst distractions are, you can time them selectively or time all Internet browsing collectively. We'll talk more about software in a later chapter on tools.

8.   Alternate connection and disconnection. There are any number of variations on this theme, but let's say

you disconnected for twenty minutes, connected for a maximum of ten minutes, and kept alternating in those intervals. Or you work disconnected for forty-five minutes and connect for fifteen minutes. You get the idea—it's almost as if the connected period is a reward for doing good, focused work.

9. Disconnect away from work. A good policy is to leave your work behind when you're done with work. A better policy is to stay disconnected during that time away from work, or work and browsing will creep into the rest of your life. Draw a *hard line* and say, "After 5:00 p.m. I won't be connected; I will focus on my family."

"The field of consciousness is tiny. It accepts only one problem at a time."
—*Antoine de Saint-Exupery*

Parents might have the most difficult challenges when it comes to finding focus. Whether you're working all day and coming home to your children, or you stay home taking care of all the household needs and very demanding children all day, there's almost never a quiet moment, almost never a time when you can relax, find focus, attain inner peace.

Leo Babauta, the author of the book *Focus*, is the father of six children, so he knows children tend to turn up the volume on life and increase the chaos of this already chaotic world by an order of several magnitudes. And while he finds that it gets easier as children get older, it never gets easy—they still need you to drive them to and from a million places, help them with a million problems, meet their basic needs and more. Chaos and work are some of the joys of being a parent. But what if we want to find focus and still be awesome parents? There's the challenge, and Leo Babauta offers a short guide to doing just that.

The Challenges

The biggest challenge is that parents wear many hats: we have jobs, have a household to run with its unending tasks, have personal things to do (workout, read, hobbies, etc.), possibly have civic commitments (volunteer, serve on a board, work with the PTA, etc.), and yes, we have children to raise.

How do we balance these commitments? How do we find focus in one, when we are constantly being pulled at by the others? In my life, for example, I try to focus on work but have children in my home office who want my attention. When I spend time with them, there's the temptation to check e-mail or Twitter. When I want to spend time alone, the siren call of work and the never-ending call of my children make focusing on my solo activity a challenge.

Technology presents yet another challenge. Parents these days are connected more than ever. Not only are we online more than ever before, we now have devices that keep us connected wherever we go: iPhones and Androids and Blackberries and iPads and laptops and iPod touches. While our teenager is texting us, we're getting work e-mails and requests from our civic commitments, or a notification of a blog post about our favorite hobby.

Children make a parent's attempt to find focus a bigger challenge than usual. People without children aren't likely to understand this, so we're not given breaks by our bosses or colleagues. Saying that you had to take your kid to the dentist, or that your baby kept you up all night crying, isn't likely to get you off the hook. After all, we signed up to be parents, didn't we?

Still, it's uniquely difficult: there isn't a minute, it seems, when our children don't need something, or have a problem, or want attention, or have an appointment or practice they need to be taken to. And if there are moments when they're not requiring our attention, often we're thinking about things we need to be doing with them or for them. We're thinking about what we should be doing but aren't: reading to them more, taking them to parks to play, teaching them to build or garden or write, working on craft projects, taking them to museums, handing down the key lessons in life. It isn't easy. But you knew that.

You'll also need to be flexible. It can be a problem when someone is so fixed on a daily routine that disruptions to the routine—a last minute meeting, a call from the school that your child is sick—will cause anxiety. As parents, of course, we learn to adapt and deal with interruptions and changes. We need to calmly accept changes to our schedule, but as we switch to a new role (parenting, work, personal, civic, etc.), we need to learn to do only that role to the extent possible.

Very Young Children

We should note that it's harder for parents of babies and toddlers. The younger the child, in general, the more demanding of your attention the child can be. It's not a hard-and-fast rule, but it gets easier to focus on other things as the child gets older.

So how do you segregate roles and find focus when your child is young and always demands your attention? It's not easy, we'll say that. The best solution involves both parents pitching in, and giving the other a break once or twice a day. So instead of both parents taking care of the child, they take turns, and one gets some quiet time for a walk, reading, work, creating, hobbies, or exercise. Then they switch.

Of course, there are also naptimes. If your baby is so young that you're not getting very much sleep, you'll probably want to rest when your baby rests. Otherwise, take advantage of naptimes and get some "you" stuff done. Take advantage of the quiet times, too, in the early morning before your child is awake, and at night when the child has gone to sleep.

Another solution is to get help: a professional babysitter, day care for half a day, one of your parents who might be retired, or a niece or nephew who is trustworthy and has a couple hours after school. While some of these solutions will cost some money, it might be worth the expense. You might also find another parent who needs help, and swap babysitting. Babysitting co-ops are also very helpful.

Support Group

Separation and divorce is usually the most painful and stressful experience a person will ever face. It's a confusing time when you feel isolated and have lots of questions about issues you've never faced before. Attending a support group for people going through a divorce can help you face the challenges of separation and divorce and move toward rebuilding your life. We recommend a group called DivorceCare. Each DivorceCare group session starts with a video seminar featuring top experts on divorce and recovery subjects. These videos feature expert interviews, real-life case studies and on-location video. After viewing video, the DivorceCare group participants spend time as a support group, discussing what was presented in that week's video seminar and what is going on in the lives of group members. Call 800-489-7778 or visit www.divorcecare.org.

Chapter 43

CONCLUSION

If you would like to discuss any area of this book in greater detail, please do not hesitate to call our office to set up an appointment. As you read this book, make notes directly in the book so we may discuss your concerns and ensure that you understand the process. We are happy to meet with our clients as often as they want. Hopefully this book will answer a lot of your preliminary questions, assist in keeping attorney's fees to a minimum, and give you a better understanding of the divorce process.

We work as a team. The more information you give us and the more organized you are, the better your chances will be to survive this period in your life with dignity. It is your responsibility to let us know how we can make your family law matters easier.

Chapter 44

GLOSSARY OF LEGAL TERMS

1. Affidavit. An affidavit is a statement of facts that is verified by one of the parties and submitted to the court in support of a motion or an order.

2. Agreed parenting plan. An agreed parenting plan is an agreement between parties in a suit affecting parent-child relationship that sets out agreed-upon terms for conservatorship, possession and access, and child support for the child.

3. Agreement or stipulation. An agreement is a formal written document between the parties and their attorneys. It can cover any subject and can used by the parties to agree on the provisions of a final judgment.

4. Alimony. Payments made to support a current or former spouse. It is also called maintenance or spousal support.

5.   Appeal. A procedure to ask a higher court to review the ruling of a lower court.

6.   Arbitration. Submitting a disputed matter for decision to a person who is not a judge. The decision of an arbitrator is usually binding and final.

7.   Associate judge: A person appointed by the presiding judge of a court who may hear any aspect of a suit over which that court has jurisdiction.

8.   Ancillary hearing. Any hearing other than the trial. It is also sometimes called a preliminary hearing.

9.   Bailiff. The person responsible for maintaining decorum in the court, similar to a sheriff.

10. Bench trial. A trial where the judge determines all facts and issues and there is no jury.

11. Case in chief. The testimony and evidence offered by one side in support of that side's positions.

12. Chambers. The judge's office.

13. Common-law marriage. A marriage without license or ceremony recognized by the law of the state in which it was created.

14. Contempt of court. Failure to comply with a court order by a person who is able to comply. It also includes conduct

in court that obstructs a court in the administration of justice.

15.   Counterclaim. The counterclaim is identical to the petition except that it is filed by the respondent against the petitioner. The respondent may claim that he or she had grounds for divorce from the petitioner that he or she wished the court to consider.

16.   Clerk. One of the persons who handles the paperwork of the court.

17.   Closing statements. These are the final statements by each attorney at the end of the trial, when each summarizes the evidence and law to persuade the court to rule in favor of his or her client.

18.   Court. A tribunal with the authority to adjudicate legal disputes between parties and carry out the administration of justice in civil, criminal and administrative matters in accordance with the rule of law. Often used interchangeably with judge.

19.   Court reporter. The person who records the testimony and court proceedings.

20.   Cross-examination. Questions asked of witnesses called by the opposing attorney.

21.   Custody. Usually refers to the parent's right to (1) have a child live with that parent; (2) make decisions concerning the child, and (3) receive child support.

This parent is called the primary joint managing conservator.

22.   Decree of divorce. The final order that is signed by the judge disposing of all issues in a suit for divorce. It is sometimes called the final judgment.

23.   Default. Failure to do something or to do it on time. For example, a default judgment applies if a respondent is served and fails to file an answer.

24.   Deposition. A deposition is testimony given under oath. The deponent is asked questions by the opposing attorney and in some cases by his or her own attorneys. The questions and answers are recorded by an official court reporter. There is little difference between testimony at a deposition and testimony in the courtroom, except that at a deposition there is no judge or rulings over matters as they arise.

25.   Direct examination. Questions asked of witnesses by the attorney who called the witness to give testimony.

26.   Discovery. Procedures used to learn facts necessary to settle a case or prepare it for trial.

27.   Evidence. Proof presented at a hearing, which includes testimony, documents, or objects.

28.   Exhibits. Tangible things presented at trial as evidence.

29.   Ex parte. Any application to a court for relief made when only one side is present, or, in some states, without formal notice.

30. Final judgment. The final order that is signed by the judge disposing of all issues. It is sometimes called a final decree of divorce or order in suit affecting parent child relationship.

31. Hearing. Any proceeding before a judicial officer.

32. Injunction. A court order that requires a party to do some act or prohibits a party from doing some act.

33. Invoking the rule. The process of requiring all witnesses, other than parties, to leave the courtroom and not discuss their testimony with anyone but the attorneys involved.

34. Informal settlement agreement (ISA). A written settlement agreement resolving issues in a divorce memorializing an agreement reached through one or more informal settlement conferences signed by all parties.

35. Interrogatories. Interrogatories are written questions directed to the other party or parties regarding finances or other relevant information. They are used in preparation for trial to obtain information not otherwise available. Interrogatories must be answered under oath by the party to whom they are directed.

36. Joint custody. Any arrangement that gives both parents legal responsibility for the care of a child. In Texas parents are appointed joint managing conservator as long as it is in the best interest of the child.

37. Jury box. The place where the jurors sit during the trial.

38.   Mediated settlement agreement (MSA). The written
        agreement made between the parties settling the issues
        in a divorce. If the document is signed at mediation by
        all parties and attorneys, it is binding and not subject to
        revocation.

39.   Modification. A change in the judgment setting out terms
        for conservatorship, periods of possession and support for a
        child based on a change of circumstances.

40.   Motion. This is a written request that the court make an
        order. A hearing will be held to determine whether or not
        the motion should be granted. It is most often used shortly
        after the divorce action has commenced for the purpose of
        obtaining a temporary order regarding custody, visitation,
        support, and other matters. It may also be used to obtain a
        change in a previous court order or judgment to commence
        contempt proceedings for failure to abide by previous
        orders.

41.   Nonresponsive. A witness's reply to a question that
        goes beyond the limits of the question and volunteers
        information.

42.   Objection. Notice to the judge by one attorney that the
        proceedings are objectionable for some reason, which the
        attorney wants to bring to the attention of the judge and
        request a ruling. If the judge disagrees, the objection is
        overruled. If the judge agrees with the objection, it is sustained.

43.   Opening statement. A brief statement by an attorney of his
        or her client's position on the issues and applicable law. It is
        generally given at the beginning of a trial.

44.   Order. Ruling by the court.

45.   Paternity. The legal relationship between a father and a child.

46.   Petition. The document filed with the Court which intiates the law suit and requests the Court to take action. In a divorce, the petition sets forth many statistical facts about the marriage and the parties and also states that the marriage is irretrievably broken. The petition is served with the summons.

47.   Petitioner. The party who initially brings or files the divorce action. Opposite party to respondent.

48.   Pleading. A document filed with the court that asks for something or responds to a pleading filed by the other party.

49.   Preliminary hearing. Any hearing other than the trial. Sometimes called ancillary hearing.

50.   Pro se. Describes a party who is representing himself or herself in a lawsuit.

51.   Rebuttal. Testimony that rebuts or refutes prior testimony.

52.   Recess. A period of time when court is not in session.

53.   Rendition. The pronouncement of the court's final ruling, which may be oral or written.

54.   Respondent. The party against whom the divorce or suit affecting parent-child relationship is initially filed. Opposite party to the petitioner.

55.   Response. The respondent may deny the marriage is irretrievably broken. Normally this must be done within twenty days after the petition is served.

56.   SAPCR. Suit affecting parent-child relationship. A lawsuit in which the Court makes a determination on conservatorship, periods of possession and support for a minor child or children.

57.   Separate property. Property that is not community that is obtained by gift, devise, or descent, or was owned prior to marriage.

58.   Service. The delivery of official papers by means prescribed by law.

59.   Settlement. The resolution of disputed issues by agreement between the parties.

60.   Stipulation. Agreement between the parties or their lawyers that is binding.

61.   Subpoena. A document served on a witness ordering that person to appear at a certain time and place to testify and/or bring designated documents.

62.   Swearing in. When a witness takes the witness oath to tell the truth. The judge will say something similar to, "Do you swear to tell the truth and nothing but the truth, so help you God?"

63.   Summons. The summons is used to begin the divorce action. It must be personally served upon the respondent.

If the respondent cannot be located, the action is started by publishing the summons in the local newspaper.

64. Temporary orders. This is an order of the court setting forth the rules that are effective prior to the final hearing of the divorce. It usually covers such items as custody, visitation, support, temporary attorney fees, temporary use of the home and other property of the parties, and payment of bills and mortgages.

65. Trial. The final hearing that decides all issues of the case.

66. Uncontested divorce. A divorce in which there is no dispute as to how any of the issues will be resolved.

67. Under advisement. A period of time after the trial during which the judge considers the testimony, evidence, and his or her notes and makes a final decision about the issues.

68. Visitation. The right of a parent who does not have primary custody of the child to spend time with the child.

69. Witness stand. The place from which the witness testifies.

Chapter 45

REQUIRED SEMINARS FOR DIVORCES INVOLVING CHILDREN

A ll parents must attend a required four-hour seminar if there are children involved in the divorce. These seminars may be required even if the divorce is uncontested. Please check with your attorney's office. Most judges will not grant a divorce if both parents have not attended one of these classes. You can meet this seminar requirement by attending any of the classes listed below. All of these seminars require a fee at registration. These seminars may be required by the court in modification cases involving child custody, visitation, or adoptions.

Galveston County

For Kids' Sake Seminar www.cogalveston.tx.us/kids_sake/default. html. Fee, forty to fifty dollars. Offered several times a month in Galveston and Texas City. Parents need to register at least forty-eight hours in advance of the class. You can obtain a class schedule and registration form from the Galveston County Law Library, Galveston County Justice Center, or by calling (409) 765-2601.

Offers weekend programs.

Consider the Children www.considerthechildren.net. Seminars offered in Houston. Twenty dollars per person. A certificate of attendance will be given to each participant at the end of class. You do not need to make an appointment. Contact (281) 481-2711.

Harris County

1.	Children Cope	713-952-2673
2.	Escape	713-942-9500
3.	Children in the Middle	713-468-8356
4.	Parents Apart	281-333-5866
5.	Family Education Institute	713-688-9122
6.	Safe Family Programs	713-755-5625
7.	DePelchin	713-730-2335
8.	Positive Parenting through Divorce	866-778-3349
	Online Parent Class: www.positiveparentingonline.com	
9.	For Kids' Sake	979-285-2061
10.	ASI Parenting Course	281-491-5001
11.	Stop the Conflict, located in Houston	713-520-5370

Online Seminars availabe for Harris County. Some Harris County courts many not accept online course.

12.   Parenting Choice. $39.99 as of 2015. You can print out your own certificate.
www.parentingchoice.com

13.   Positive Parenting through Divorce. $60.00 as of 2015. Your certificate will be mailed.
www.positiveparentingthroughdivorce.com

14.   Parenting Partnerships. $65.00 as of 2015. You can print your own certificate upon completion.
www.parentingpartnerships.com

Fort Bend County

Please note: Fort Bend County accepts only the following parent education courses.

1. Escape Family Resource Center, Families and Divorce 713-942-9500
2. DePelchin Children's Center   713-730-2335
3. Divorce as Friends, Stop the Conflict   713-520-5370

Online courses available for Fort Bend County

4. www.ucrecovery.com
5. www.puttingkidsfirst.org
6. www.kidsfirsttexas.com
7. www.family-affairs.org
8. www.parentingchoice.com
9. www.txparent.com
10. www.parentclassonline.com
11. www.onlineparentingprograms.com
12. www.parentingpartnerships.com

Montgomery County

1. Children Cope with Divorce, locations in Richmond and Houston, 713-952-COPE
2. Escape Family Resource Center, locations in Richmond and Houston, 713-942-9500
3. DePelchin Children's Center, locations in Stafford and Houston, 713-730-2335
4. Divorce as Friends, Stop the Conflict, Houston, 713-520-5370

Exhibit No. 1
FINANCIAL INFORMATION SHEET

CAUSE NO. 1234-56789   JUDICIAL DISTRICT COURT

1.   Date of Marriage: 01/01/2000
2.   Date of Separation: 01/01/2014
3.   Custody of the children is presently with Mother
4.   Age of children: 11 and 12
5.   My monthly expenses are:

Mortgage or Rent	1,000	Tuition (College Fund)	25
Utilities	300	Lunches/Supplies	30
Food	500	Haircuts	30
Doctor/Dentist/Drugs	150	Clothing	50
Car Insurance Payment	180	Cleaning/Laundry	20
Car Payment	300	Gifts	100
Gasoline/Oil/Parking	100	Church Support	100
Car Maintenance	50	Health Insurance	150
Cell Phone	100		
SubTotal	2,680	**Total**	**3,185**

Credit Cards	Total	Monthly Payment
BOA Visa	3,000	120

TOTAL MONTHLY EXPENSES: $3,305.00

6.   I am currently employed at ABC Company. Based on my last paystub, my monthly earnings are:

Gross Income: 4,166.67
Withholding Tax: 484.92
Medicare and Soc. Sec.   318.75
Other(list)deductions: 0.00
NET MONTHLY: 3,363.00

7.   Quick Assets I have control of:

Cash	$100	Undeposited checks	$0
Banks	$1,500	Stocks/Bonds	$0
Credit Union	$0	401K	$30,000

I, the undersigned, do hereby certify that the foregoing answers are true and correct to the best of my knowledge.

DATE _____   SIGNATURE _____

EXHIBIT 2

HUSBAND'S INVENTORY AND APPRAISEMENT AND
PROPOSED PROPERTY DIVISION

#	PROPERTY		EQUITY	HUSBAND	WIFE
1	Residence (150,000-100,000)		50,000		50,000
2	Wells Fargo Checking Acct #5678	H	10,000	10,000	
3	Wells Fargo Savings Acct #7890	H	1,000	1,000	
4	Chase Checking Acct #1234	W	5,000		5,000
5	Chase Savings Acct #4123	W	0		0
6	Americatrade 401k	H	100,000	100,000	
7	Retirement 401k	W	50,000		50,000
8	IRA	W	25,000		25,000
9	Vehicle	W	10,000		10,000
10	Vehicle	H	20,000	20,000	
11	Bonus	H	Unknown	50%	50%
12.	Furniture & Personal Property		10,000	5,000	5,000
	COMMUNITY LIABILITIES				
13	Attorney Fees	H	1,500	1,500	
14	Attorney Fees	W	1,500		1,500
15	Joint IRS Liability		Unknown	50%	50%
16	School Loans		Each	Pay	Own
17	Property Taxes		5,000		5,000
18	Credit cards	H	1,000	1,000	
19	Credit cards	W	5,000		5,000
	ASSET TOTAL		281,000	136,000	145,000
	LIABILITIES TOTAL		14,000	2,500	11,500
	NET COMMUNITY ESTATE		267,000	133,500	133,500
	Percentage of Community Estate		**100%**	**50.00%**	**50.00%**

1

VERIFICATION TO INVENTORY AND APPRAISEMENT

I, _____, state on oath that, to the best of my knowledge and belief, this inventory

and appraisement contains-

1. a full and complete list of all properties that I claim belong to the community estate of me and my spouse, with the values thereof;
2. a full and complete list of all properties in my possession or subject to my control that I claim or admit are my or my spouse's separate property and estate, with the values thereof; and
3. a full and complete list of the debts that I claim are community indebtedness.

Any omission from this inventory is not intentional but is done through mere inadvertence and

not to mislead my spouse. There may be other assets and liabilities of which my spouse is

aware, and the omission of those items from this inventory should not be construed as a waiver

of my interest in them.

_____
Husband or Wife

THE STATE OF TEXAS   §
                         §
COUNTY OF_____   §

SIGNED under oath before me on _____

_____
Notary Public, State of Texas

2

EXHIBIT 3

RECOMMENDED READING

If you read a book that was beneficial, please email it so I may add it to my recommended reading list.

Anger Busting 101: The New ABC's for Angry Men and The Women Who Love Them, Newton Hightower. Best book on learning how to deal with anger. It changed my life.

Seven Choices, by Elizabeth Harper Neeld, Ph.D. 1990
 A comprehensive guide to dealing with the stages of change in life, whether from divorce or death. A well-researched, written book offering valuable insights and shared experiences.

Spiritual Divorce, by Debbie Ford, HarperCollins Publishers, 2001
This book explains how to make your divorce a catalyst for an extraordinary life.

Sharing the Children, How to resolve Custody Problems and Get on With Your Life, by Robert E. Adler, Ph.D., Adler & Adler, Publishers, 1988.
 Focuses on the needs of the children after divorce. Deciding custody, vitiation and positive negotiating are explored in an effort to reduce the pain of the separation for the children as well as the spouses. Appendices include self-help checklists, child development chart and custody rules.

The Nurturing Father, by Kyle D. Pruett, M.D., Warner books, 1987
 Examines the nurturing capacities of fathers as primary care givers-changing traditional identities of male and female roles. Explores the relationship of father and child and includes study where father is the primary care giver.

Getting Apart Together (A Couple's Guide to a Fair Divorce or Separation), by Martin A. Kranitz, Impact Publishers, 1987
 Emphasizes equity and the reduction of animosity during separation and divorce. Suggests an attitude of looking at the situation "as a problem to be solved jointly rather than a battle to be won or lost." This book included a discussion agenda, budget worksheet and more.

Second Chances, by Judith Wallerstein - Ticknor & Fields, 1989.
 A picture of divorce, based on the only ten-year longitudinal study of divorce ever conducted. An exploration of the complexities, tragedies, and opportunities inherent in divorce and an explanation of the ripple effects extending beyond the family. Especially beneficial in understanding the effects of divorce on children and how they can be minimized.

Growing Up Divorced, by Linda Bird Francke, Ballantine Books, 1983
 Written for divorced parents, the book guides them along the prevalent behavior by children of divorce. Seven of the twelve chapters are devoted to specific age groups and how at each level, children might perceive their situation emotionally and logically.

The Kids' Guide to Divorce, by John P. Brogan & Ula Maiden, Fawcett Crest, 1986
Real life experiences of kids with divorced parents, their feelings and how they cope with them. Advice on ways to deal with the vast array of emotions as well as understanding what is happening to the whole family during violence. Examples of how some kids react in given situations and then suggestions of possible alternative behaviors that could have been used to deal with the situation in a healthier way.

Divorce Book For Parents, Helping Your Children Cope With Divorce and its Aftermath, by Vicki Lansky, New American Library, 1989
Begins with the initial separation of parents, moves though the legal process and options of custody and ends with suggestions on how to handle explicit scenarios such as family gatherings and dating. A easy to read, nuts-bolts guide which also lists the addresses and phone numbers of several support organizations.

Husbands & Wives A Guide To Solving Problems and Building Relationships

Debt-Free Living (How to Get Out of Debt and Stay Out by Larry Burkett
This book talks about how common it is for money problems to be at the heart of marriage problems and how to resolve them.

You Can Heal Your Heart by Greg Kessler and Louise Hay.
A book on how to grief and heal yourself after a loss.

I Can Do It by Louise Hay.
Nurtures you to change your learned childhood habits and obtain the confidence to attain the life you really deserve.

Book Perfect Pictures by Christy Whitman.
Explains how we perceive perfection and the impact it has in our lives, our spouses, jobs and friends.

Jump...and your life will appear by Nancy Levin
The author shares the belief that what we believe to be true, even though not true will become true because we allow it.

Children's Books

Why are we Getting a Divorce? by Peter Mayle, Harmony Books, 1988
Intended to be read by a parent to the younger child, this book explores reasons why parents' divorce and how life changed because of it. The book suggests ways to make life a little easier by focusing on recovery rather than sadness and alleviating family stress.

The Boys and Girls Book About Divorce, (For Children & Their Divorced Parents) by Robert A Gardner, M.D.
Recommended for parents and children with good reading skills. Focuses on how children can handle problems. Based on real situations that have come up for children of divorced homes,

this is a self-help book for children on how to deal with their divorced parents.

Dinosaur's Divorce, A Guide for Changing Families, by Laurence Kransy Brown & March Brown, Joy Street Books, 1986, Little Brown & Co,.
For every young reader, this picture book is easy to read and understand. The colorful make believe dinosaur families who have divorced help illustrate common feelings and typical situations that children of divorced parents experience. Highly recommended.

Exhibit 4

ALLISON JONES & ASSOCIATES P.C.
Attorneys and Counselors at Law
1526 Heights Boulevard
Houston, Texas 77008
BOARD CERTIFIED - FAMILY LAW
Office: 713-861-7777Facsimile: 713-861-1010

January 1, 2014

John Doe   Invoice # 1234
567 Happy Road
Houston, Texas 77009

In Reference To: Divorce/Custody Case

BALANCE DUE IN FULL 15 DAYS AFTER RECEIPT OF INVOICE

Professional Services

			Hours	Amount
12/1/10 AJ		Initial Intake	1.0	425.00
	MLP	Drafted Original Petition	1.25	156.25
	MLP	Call from Client	.25	31.25
	AJ	Call to opposing to set settlement conference	.25	106.25
		For Professional Services Rendered		718.75

Outside Expenses

Harris County District Court	275.00
Nelson's Process Service	125.00
For Outside Expenses	400.00
Total Amount of this Bill	1,118.75
Retainer	(2,500.00)
Trust Account Balance	1,381.25

Current	30 Days	60 Days	90 Days	120+ Days

(1,381.25)

Exhibit 5

Cause No. _____

	§	
_____	§	_____DISTRICT COURT
VS.	§	
_____	§	HARRIS COUNTY, TEXAS

SCHEDULING ORDER and NOTICE OF INTENT TO DISMISS

*** ALL DEADLINES ARE PRIOR TO TRIAL SETTING DATE ***

** Rule 11 Agreements will NOT delay trial date **

1. PRIOR TO TRIAL **PARENT EDUCATION PROGRAM.** Parents shall file with the court proof of completion of an approved parent education program by this date (if visitation and/or custody is an issue).

2. PRIOR TO TRIAL **ALTERNATIVE DISPUTE RESOLUTION (ADR).** By this date the parties must either (a) FILE AN AGREEMENT FOR ADR, STATING THE FORM OF ADR AND THE NAME OF AN AGREED MEDIATOR, if applicable, or (b) set an objection to ADR. If no timely agreement or objection is filed, the court may sign an ADR order.

3. TRCP **INVENTORY AND APPRAISEMENT.** Spouses shall exchange a sworn Inventory and Appraisement prepared in conformity with Local Rule 4.4 by this date. Compliance with this paragraph is not a substitute for the requirements in Local Rule 4.3. All supplements must be filed 10 days prior to trial setting.

4. TRCP **JOINDER.** All parties must be added and served, whether by amendment or third party practice by this date. THE PARTY CAUSING THE JOINDER SHALL PROVIDE A COPY OF THIS SCHEDULING ORDER AT THE TIME OF SERVICE.

5. TRCP **DISCOVERY.** All discovery requests and deposition notices must be filed by this date. Discovery may be initiated after this date by stipulation in conformity with Rule 11, Tex. Rules of Civil Procedure. Incomplete discovery will not delay the trial date.

6. TRCP **PLEADINGS.** All amendments and supplements must be filed by this date. This order does not preclude prompt filing of pleadings directly responsive to any timely filed pleadings.

NOTICE OF INTENT TO DISMISS ON TRIAL DATE. THIS CASE WILL BE DISMISSED FOR WANT OF PROSECUTION if, prior to the trial setting there is no:

    a. **Service with citation; or**
    b. **Answer on file, after proper service with citation, and no default judgment signed; or**
    c. **Properly executed Waiver on file;**
    d. **Mediation completed.**

7. **PRETRIAL CONFERENCE at** _____ Set by court or upon motion.

8. _____ **TRIAL** at 9:00 am THIS CASE IS SET FOR TRIAL ON THE MERITS ON THIS DATE. If not assigned by the second Friday after this date, this case will be reset.

SIGNED _____

_____
JUDGE PRESIDING

Exhibit 6

JANE DOE, JUDGE

999TH JUDICIAL DISTRICT COURT
CIVIL JUSTICE CENTER 20TH FLOOR
201 CAROLINE ST.
HOUSTON, TEXAS 77002
(713) 555-5555

NOTICE OF INTENT TO DISMISS FOR WANT OF PROSECUTION

THE BELOW CAPTIONED CASE HAS BEEN SET FOR A HEARING TO DISMISS FOR WANT OF PROSECUTION ON:

January 3, 2014 at 9:00 a.m.

IN THE 999TH DISTRICT COURT, 20TH FLOOR, 201 CAROLINE ST., HOUSTON, TEXAS 77002

FAILURE TO APPEAR WILL RESULT IN DISMISSAL FOR WANT OF PROSECUTION ON THAT DATE IN ACCORDANCE WITH THE PROVISIONS OF T.R.C.P. 165A

IF YOU HAVE ANY QUESTIONS, YOU MAY REACH THE COURT COORDINATOR AT 713-555-5555

JANE DOE
Judge, 999TH DISTRICT COURT

CASE 1234-56789   FILED – 20130103   COURT – 999th
TYPE – DIVORCE WITH CHILDREN

Exhibit 7

Standard Possession Order

One of the biggest issues to be resolved is the schedule for periods of possession of the child. The Texas Legislature has provided by statute what is called the Standard Possession Order. This is a possession schedule for periods of possession for the non-primary parent. Many of the provisions of the Standard Possession Order are based on the child's school schedule. If the child is not in school, then the schedule is based on the schedule for the school district where the child lives.

Most possession schedules start out by stating that the parents will have possession of the child at all times mutually agreed to by the parents, and in absence of an agreement, under the terms of the Order. This language is included so that parents can work together on accommodating each other's schedules and cooperate with each other so that they both are able to spend time with the child. There will always be reasons for parents to want to deviate from the schedule in the Order, like family events, work responsibilities and unexpected emergencies. Parents are encouraged to cooperate with each other when these circumstances come up for the benefit of the children involved.

For easier reading convenience the following schedule assumes Mother has custody, but will be reversed when Dad is awarded custody.

Standard Possession Order

The Court finds that the following provisions of this Standard Possession Order are intended to and do comply with the requirements of Texas Family Code sections 153.311 through 153.317. IT IS ORDERED that this Standard Possession Order is effective immediately.

a. Definitions

1. In this Standard Possession Order "school" means the primary or secondary school in which the child is enrolled or, if the child is not enrolled in a primary or secondary school, the public school district in which the child primarily resides.

2. In this Standard Possession Order "child" includes each child, whether one or more, who is a subject of this suit while that child is under the age of eighteen years and not otherwise emancipated.

IT IS ORDERED that the conservators shall have possession of the child at times mutually agreed to in advance by the parties, and, in the absence of mutual agreement, it is ORDERED that the conservators shall have possession of the child under the specified terms set out in this Standard Possession Order.

Parents Who Reside 100 Miles or Less Apart

Except as otherwise explicitly provided in this Standard Possession Order, when Dad resides 100 miles or less from the primary residence of the child, Dad shall have the right to possession of the child as follows:

1. Weekends—On weekends, beginning at 6:00 P.M., on the first, third, and fifth Friday of each month and ending at 6:00 P.M. on the following Sunday.

2. Weekend Possession Extended by a Holiday—Except as otherwise explicitly provided in this Standard Possession Order, if a weekend period of possession by Dad begins on a Friday that is a school holiday during the regular school term or a federal, state, or local holiday during the summer months when school is not in session, or if the period ends on or is immediately followed by a Monday that is such a holiday, that weekend period of possession shall begin at 6:00 P.M. on the Thursday immediately preceding the Friday holiday or school holiday or end at 6:00 P.M. on that Monday holiday or school holiday, as applicable.

3. Thursdays—On Thursday of each week during the regular school term, beginning at 6:00 P.M. and ending at 8:00 P.M.

4. Spring Break in Even-Numbered Years—In even-numbered years, beginning at 6:00 P.M. on the day the child is dismissed from school for the school's spring vacation and ending at 6:00 P.M. on the day before school resumes after that vacation.

5. Extended Summer Possession by Dad—With Written Notice by April 1—If Dad gives Mom written notice by April 1 of a year specifying an extended period or periods of summer possession for that year, Dad shall have possession of the child for thirty days beginning no earlier than the day after the child's school is dismissed for the summer vacation and ending no later than seven days before school resumes at the end of the summer vacation in that year, to be exercised in no more than two separate periods of at least seven consecutive days each, as specified in the written notice. These periods of possession shall begin and end at 6:00 p.m.

    Without Written Notice by April 1—If Dad does not give Mom written notice by April 1 of a year specifying an extended period or periods of summer possession for that year, Dad shall have possession of the child for thirty consecutive days in that year beginning at 6:00 P.M. on July 1 and ending at 6:00 P.M. on July 31.

Notwithstanding the weekend and Thursday periods of possession ORDERED for Dad, it is explicitly ORDERED that Mom shall have a superior right of possession of the child as follows:

1. Spring Break in Odd-Numbered Years—In odd-numbered years, beginning at 6:00 P.M. on the day the child is dismissed from school for the school's spring vacation and ending at 6:00 P.M. on the day before school resumes after that vacation.

2

2. Summer Weekend Possession by Mom —If Mom gives Dad written notice by April 15 of a year, Mom shall have possession of the child on any one weekend beginning at 6:00 P.M. on Friday and ending at 6:00 P.M. on the following Sunday during any one period of the extended summer possession by Dad in that year, provided that Mom picks up the child from Dad and returns the child to that same place.

3. Extended Summer Possession by Mom —If Mom gives Dad written notice by April 15 of a year or gives Dad fourteen days' written notice on or after April 16 of a year, Mom may designate one weekend beginning no earlier than the day after the child's school is dismissed for the summer vacation and ending no later than seven days before school resumes at the end of the summer vacation, during which an otherwise scheduled weekend period of possession by Dad shall not take place in that year, provided that the weekend so designated does not interfere with Dad's summer possession or Father's Day.

Parents Who Reside More Than 100 Miles Apart

Except as otherwise explicitly provided in this Standard Possession Order, when Dad resides more than 100 miles from the residence of the child, Dad shall have the right to possession of the child as follows:

1. Weekends—Unless Dad elects the alternative period of weekend possession described in the next paragraph, Dad shall have the right to possession of the child on weekends, beginning at 6:00 P.M. on the first, third, and fifth Friday of each month and ending at 6:00 P.M. on the following Sunday. Except as otherwise explicitly provided in this Standard Possession Order, if such a weekend period of possession by Dad begins on a Friday that is a school holiday during the regular school term or a federal, state, or local holiday during the summer months when school is not in session, or if the period ends on or is immediately followed by a Monday that is such a holiday, that weekend period of possession shall begin at 6:00 P.M. on the Thursday immediately preceding the Friday holiday or school holiday or end at 6:00 P.M. on that Monday holiday or school holiday, as applicable.

Alternate Weekend Possession—In lieu of the weekend possession described in the foregoing paragraph, Dad shall have the right to possession of the child not more than one weekend per month of Dad's choice beginning at 6:00 P.M. on the day school recesses for the weekend and ending at 6:00 P.M. on the day before school resumes after the weekend. Except as otherwise explicitly provided in this Standard Possession Order, if such a weekend period of possession by Dad begins on a Friday that is a school holiday during the regular school term or a federal, state, or local holiday during the summer months when school is not in session, or if the period ends on or is immediately followed by a Monday that is such a holiday, that weekend period of possession shall begin at 6:00 P.M. on the Thursday immediately preceding the Friday holiday or school holiday or end at 6:00 P.M. on that Monday holiday or school holiday, as applicable. Dad may elect an option for this alternative period of weekend possession by giving written notice to Mom within ninety days after the parties begin to reside more than 100 miles apart. If Dad makes this election, Dad shall give Mom fourteen days' written or telephonic notice preceding a designated weekend. The weekends chosen shall not conflict with the provisions regarding Christmas, Thanksgiving, the child's birthday, and Mother's Day Weekend below.

2. Spring Break in All Years—Every year, beginning at 6:00 P.M. on the day the child is dismissed from school for the school's spring vacation and ending at 6:00 P.M. on the day before school resumes after that vacation.

3. Extended Summer Possession by Dad—With Written Notice by April 1ˢᵗ—If Dad gives Mom written notice by April 1 of a year specifying an extended period or periods of summer possession for that year, Dad shall have possession of the child for forty-two days beginning no earlier than the day after the child's school is dismissed for the summer vacation and ending no later than seven days before school resumes at the end of the summer vacation in that year, to be exercised in no more than two separate periods of at least seven consecutive days each, as specified in the written notice. These periods of possession shall begin and end at 6:00 P.M.

    Without Written Notice by April 1—If Dad does not give Mom written notice by April 1 of a year specifying an extended period or periods of summer possession for that year, Dad shall have possession of the child for forty-two consecutive days beginning at 6:00 P.M. on June 15 and ending at 6:00 P.M. on July 27 of that year.

Notwithstanding the weekend periods of possession ORDERED for Dad, it is explicitly ORDERED that Mom shall have a superior right of possession of the child as follows:

1. Summer Weekend Possession by Mom—If Mom gives Dad written notice by April 15 of a year, Mom shall have possession of the child on any one weekend beginning at 6:00 P.M. on Friday and ending at 6:00 P.M. on the following Sunday during any one period of possession by Dad during Dad's extended summer possession in that year, provided that if a period of possession by Dad in that year exceeds thirty days, Mom may have possession of the child under the terms of this provision on any two nonconsecutive weekends during that period and provided that Mom picks up the child from Dad and returns the child to that same place and that the weekend so designated does not interfere with Father's Day Weekend.

2. Extended Summer Possession by Mom—If Mom gives Dad written notice by April 15 of a year, Mom may designate twenty-one days beginning no earlier than the day after the child's school is dismissed for the summer vacation and ending no later than seven days before school resumes at the end of the summer vacation in that year, to be exercised in no more than two separate periods of at least seven consecutive days each, during which Dad shall not have possession of the child, provided that the period or periods so designated do not interfere with Dad's period or periods of extended summer possession or with Father's Day Weekend.

Holidays Unaffected by Distance

Notwithstanding the weekend and Thursday periods of possession of Dad, the Parents shall have the right to possession of the child as follows:

1. Christmas Holidays in Even—Numbered Years-In even-numbered years, Dad shall have the right to possession of the child beginning 6:00 P.M. on the day the child is dismissed from school for the Christmas school vacation and ending at noon on December 28, and Mom shall have the right to possession of the child beginning at noon on December 28 and ending at 6:00 P.M. on the day before school resumes after that Christmas school vacation.

2. Christmas Holidays in Odd-Numbered Years—In odd-numbered years, Mom shall have the right to possession of the child beginning at 6:00 P.M. on the day the child is dismissed from school for the Christmas school vacation and ending at noon on December 28, and Dad shall have the right to possession of the child beginning at noon on December 28 and ending at 6:00 P.M. on the day before the child's school resumes after that Christmas school vacation.

3. Thanksgiving in Odd-Numbered Years—In odd-numbered years, Dad shall have the right to possession of the child beginning at 6:00 P.M. on the day the child is dismissed from school for the Thanksgiving holiday and ending at 6:00 P.M. on the Sunday following Thanksgiving.

4. Thanksgiving in Even-Numbered Years—In even-numbered years, Mom shall have the right to possession of the child beginning at 6:00 P.M. on the day the child is dismissed from school for the Thanksgiving holiday and ending at 6:00 P.M. on the Sunday following Thanksgiving.

5. Child's Birthday—If a conservator is not otherwise entitled under this Standard Possession Order to present possession of the a child on the child's birthday, that conservator shall have possession of the child and the child's minor siblings beginning at 6:00 P.M. and ending at 8:00 P.M. on that day, provided that conservator picks up the children from the other conservator's residence and returns the children to that same place.

6. Father's Day Weekend—Father shall have the right to possession of the child each year, beginning at 6:00 P.M. on the Friday preceding Father's Day and ending at 6:00 P.M. on Father's Day.

7. Mother's Day Weekend—Mother shall have the right to possession of the child each year, beginning at 6:00 P.M. on the Friday preceding Mother's Day and ending at 6:00 P.M. on Mother's Day.

5

Exhibit 8

Daily Events Log

May, 6   John called 15 minutes before he was supposed to pick up John Jr. to tell me he was going to be 30 minutes late. He was an hour and a half late and would not tell me why. John Jr. was in tears

May 8   John dropped John Jr. off two hours late without letting me know. He smelled like alcohol when he arrived. John Jr. arrived wearing the same clothes and hungry.

May 13   John called me and sounded drunk. He said he could not pick up John Jr. that evening. John had promised to take John Jr. to a baseball game that evening. I had to tell him that his Dad needed to reschedule.

When I told John Jr. he started to cry. I cancelled my exercise class and took him to the movies.

May 26   John was late again picking up John Jr. Going to San Antonio for the weekend to visit John Jr.'s grandparents.

May 27   John brought back John Jr. this morning. Decided against going to San Antonio. Instead going with one of his buddies who called him on the way to SA and invited him to the baseball game tonight.

June 15 Received a call from John JR.'s daycare around 9:30 a.m. informing me that he was running a temperature. I am in a business meeting in Galveston. Called John and asked if he could pick up John Jr from daycare. He agreed and said he would be there within 30 minutes. Received a call from daycare at 2:00 p.m. John Jr. was still in the school's clinic. Called John. He stated he had fallen asleep.

August 21 John had promised John Jr. he would take him to school on his first day of school. He never showed up or returned my numerous calls. I had to drive him to school and was an hour late to work.

John called at 7:00 p.m. stating that he thought school's first day was the following Monday.

August 30 Open House at John Jr's school. John Jr. had given him a homemade invitation but he still failed to appear. John Jr. kept asking where his dad was after seeing other fathers there. Took him to buy an ice cream.

Sept 25 John Jr. birthday party at Chuck E Cheese. John showed up as we were leaving. John gave his son a 20.00 bill as a birthday present.

Exhibit 9

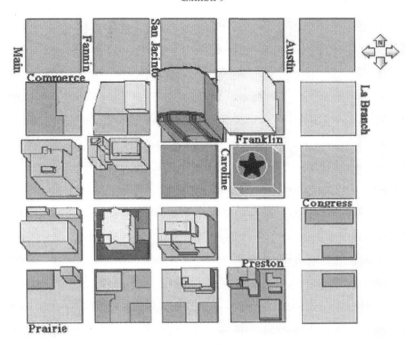

Harris County Family Law Courts
Harris County Civil Courthouse (See ★above)
201 Caroline
Houston, Texas 77002

245th Family Court
15th Floor

246th Family Court
16th Floor

247th Family Court
15th Floor

257th Family Court
16th Floor

280th Family Court
15th Floor

308th Family Court
8th Floor

309th Family Court
16th Floor

310th Family Court
15th Floor

311th Family Court
8th Floor

312th Family Court
16th Floor

To Mary Lou, Ashley, Holly, Annette, Dana, Orphie, Sylvia, and Mom:
I could not have done this without you.
Thank you for your support and encouragement.

To Mike:
Thanks for making this possible. I love our relationship.
Thanks, Allison

To Susan:
Thank you for all of your support and encouragement.

To Xander:
Thank you for giving me the proper perspective.

To Mary Lou, Ashley, Holly, Annette, Dana, and Orphie:
Thank you for all of your hard work and encouragement. We could not have done any of this without you.

Thank you, Owen.

Made in the USA
Coppell, TX
04 March 2020